Near Eastern Seals

INTERPRETING·THE·PAST

NEAR EASTERN
SEALS

Dominique Collon

University of California Press/British Museum

University of California Press
Berkeley and Los Angeles

© 1990 The Trustees of the British Museum

Designed by Andrew Shoolbred

Printed in Great Britain

**Library of Congress Cataloging-in-
Publication Data**
Collon, Dominique.
    Near   Eastern   seals / Dominique   Collon — 1st
    U.S. ed.
        p. cm. — (Interpreting the past series; 2)
    Includes index.
    ISBN 0–520–07308–8 (paper)
        1. Cylinder seals—Middle East. 2. Middle East—
    Antiquities.
    I. Title.   II. Series.
    CD5344.C59 1991
    737'.6'0956—dc20   90–40447
                                                            CIP

Cover illustration: Seals illustrated in figures
1 (A–E), 9, 18, 24 (C), 41 and **45**; and WA 22962, an
Early Dynastic lapis lazuli seal dating from about
2500 BC.

Contents

Acknowledgements   7

Preface   9

Map   10

1 Seals in the Ancient Near East   11

2 Seals, the Antiquarian and the Archaeologist   21

3 The Evidence of the Materials   31

4 The Evidence of Technical Development   39

5 The Evidence of the Designs   43

6 The Development of Glyptic Studies   55

Chronological Table   60

Index of Figure References   61

Index   62

Acknowledgements

In the preparation of this book I received help and encouragement from Celia Clear and Nina Shandloff of British Museum Publications and my colleagues in the Department of Western Asiatic Antiquities. I am grateful to Barbara Winter for the cover photograph, and to her and her colleague Lisa Bliss for many of the photographs of British Museum seals and for printing a number of others. My thanks also go to Annie Searight who drew the map. The drawings of the seals are my own.

I am grateful to the following museums, collections and individuals for allowing me to reproduce the items listed by figure number below:
Baghdad, Iraq Museum: **3** (Michael Roaf), **10** (Ur excavation archive)
Berlin, Antikenmuseum (Gertrud Platz): **16**
Berlin, Pergamonmuseum (Evelyn Klengel): **21, 29, 30**
Bodrum Museum (George Bass): **17**
Chicago, Oriental Institute Museum (John Larson): **8**
London, British Museum, Department of Western Asiatic Antiquities: **1, 2, 4, 6, 7, 9, 10** (Ur excavation archive), **12–14, 18, 19, 24, 25, 27, 32–4, 38–42, 45**
London, Institute of Archaeology (Alalakh excavation archive): **15**
New York, Jonathan Rosen Collection: **23**
New York, Metropolitan Museum of Art (Prudence Harper): **43**
Oxford, Ashmolean Museum (Roger Moorey): **35–7**
Paris, Bibliothèque Nationale (Irène Aghion): **26**
Paris, ex-De Clercq Collection: **22**
Paris, Louvre (Annie Caubet): **5** (Pierre Amiet), **11, 28** and **31** (drawings after Pierre Amiet)
Philadelphia, University Museum (Ur excavation archive): **10**
Thebes Museum (Edith Porada): **20**

Preface

Over half a million clay tablets, many of them bearing the impressions of seals, have survived from the Ancient Near East. They provide a huge archive of evidence for the period from about 3300 to 300 BC. To this can be added the information supplied by thousands of clay sealings and bullae used from the fifth millennium BC onwards. The study of all these impressions and of many thousands of original pre-Islamic seals is thus central to our understanding of 'the cradle of civilisation'.

Seals can be studied in a variety of ways and on many levels. They can be seen as *objets d'art*, and perhaps collected as an investment. They can be studied as evidence of trade patterns and routes. They can be used to chronicle changes in the administrative or legal systems in force during their long history. They can throw light on technical development in the art of cutting and boring hard and soft stones. Their role as amulets in medical and magical rituals can be examined.

The designs of seals are a fascinating record of the religious beliefs of their owners, of contemporary fashions or developments in dress, architecture, transport, music, sport, festivals, myths, patterns and iconography. They reflect the ways their owners looked at the world around them and interpreted what they saw. As such, seals enable us, in a small way, to interpret the past.

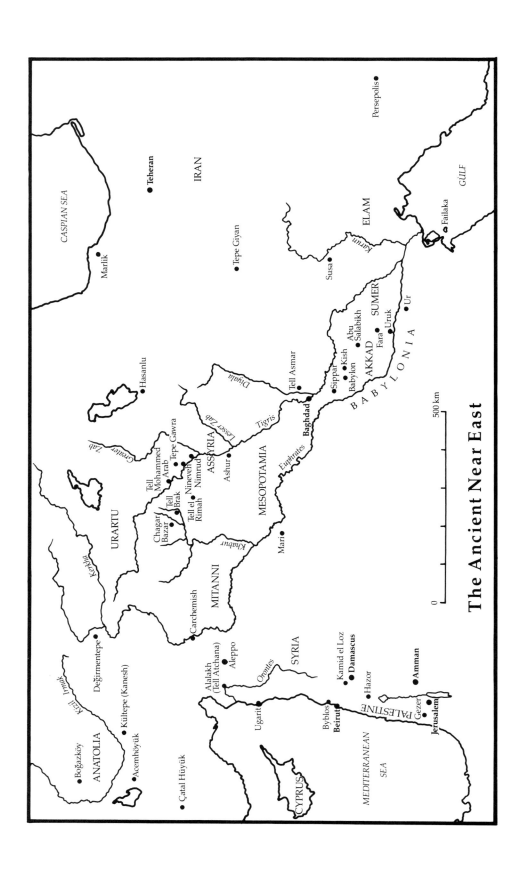

The Ancient Near East

— 1 —

Seals in the Ancient Near East

A *seal* is an object made of hard material – generally stone but sometimes bone, ivory, faience, glass, metal, wood or even sun-dried or baked clay – which is carved with a design. This design is generally recessed (carved in *intaglio*) so that when it is impressed on clay or wax it will leave an *impression* in relief (fig. 1). Very occasionally the seal is carved in relief (*cameo*) so that the impression is recessed (fig. 21). The object impressed is sometimes also referred to as a seal, but to avoid confusion it will here be called a *sealing* (fig. 2). The word *glyptic* is often used as a general term to refer to both seals and sealings.

For seven thousand years the act of sealing has guaranteed authenticity, marked ownership, indicated participation in a legal transaction, or protected goods against theft. Until fairly recently letters would be sealed with a lump of wax on which the seal bearing the owner's device was impressed; even now tags of lead bearing an official stamp are attached to the ropes or wires that secure goods going through customs. In ancient times clay was the most commonly sealed material. It was applied to the ropes or string securing bales, sacks, boxes, baskets (fig. 4), jars or storeroom doors. Sometimes specially shaped sealings were attached to objects or documents; these sealed pieces of clay are generally called *bullae* (singular: *bulla*; from the Latin, meaning a round object) and their shape and size vary according to place and period (fig. 2). In some areas and at some periods seals were also impressed on pottery at the time of manufacture (fig. 3). Many of the seals we shall be examining were impressed on clay tablets and clay envelopes associated with the earliest form of writing to be developed (figs. 13 and 15).

The earliest writing systems known are to be found along the great river systems of the world: the Tigris and Euphrates, the Nile, the Indus and the Yellow River. These major rivers linked many different regions and were the economic lifeline of the countries through which they flowed. They carried trade, and organised trade required an efficient administration. Writing was developed to fill the needs of administration and the earliest documents were lists and accounts of goods traded or stored. Seals were used to ratify such accounts, to mark ownership and to identify stores and consignments. Thus seals and writing developed together. It is generally agreed that writing first appeared in southern Iraq, ancient Mesopotamia, which means the 'Land of the Two Rivers'.

The Tigris and Euphrates rise in the highlands of eastern Anatolia (now Turkey – see map on p. 10). The Euphrates then flows west and south into Syria, south-east through Syria into Mesopotamia and finally into the Gulf. The Tigris has its source in an area famous for its copper mines, flows south into northern Mesopotamia and south-eastwards to join the Euphrates just before entering the Gulf. Both rivers have substantial left-bank tributaries and those of the Tigris – the Karun, Kerkha, Diyala and Zab rivers – stretch into western and south-western Iran. A subsidiary system is formed by the Orontes and Jordan rivers and the Wadi Araba, parallel to the Mediterranean coast in Syria and Palestine. All these areas make up what is generally referred to as the Ancient Near East, 'the cradle of civilisation'.

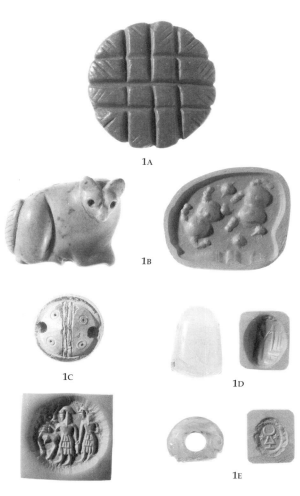

1A

1B

1C

1D

1E

A selection of stamp seals of various periods (*see* **cover illustration**).

1A Prehistoric button seal with a rectilinear design. It was found by Ernst Herzfeld at Tepe Giyan in western Iran, and probably dates to *c.* 5000 BC. Orange stone; 3.9 × 1.15 cm. London, British Museum, WA 128665.

1B Seal amulet in the shape of a fox, with its modern impression. Similar objects, perforated for suspension, have been found throughout Mesopotamia in contexts dating to the late 4th millennium BC. The drilled design on the base consists of stylised animals. Cream stone with red flecks; 2.95 × 3.6 × 1.85 cm. London, British Museum, WA 134749.

1C Late Gulf stamp seal of the beginning of the 2nd millennium BC. Such seals originated in Bahrein and Failaka in the Gulf, but several examples, of which this is one, have been found at Ur in southern Iraq. They have also been found at Susa in south-western Iran, in Bactria (present-day Afghanistan) and at Lothal on the west coast of India, and testify to an active trade network. The domed back with its triple lines and four centre-dot circles is typical of Late Gulf seals, as are the material and the way the two figures and goat are depicted. Burnt steatite; 2.2 × 1.15 cm. London, British Museum, WA 118704.

1D Conoid stamp seal of the Neo-Babylonian period (6th century BC), bearing the stylised representation of a worshipper or priest before divine symbols. Blue chalcedony; 2.3 × 1.6 × 1.3 cm. London, British Museum, WA 115528.

1E Sasanian stamp seal of the 4th century AD. The device on the base is probably a hereditary mark of ownership. Cornelian; 0.9 × 1.1 cm. London, British Museum, WA 119665.

12

2A Clay bulla bearing the impression of a Late Uruk cylinder seal (*c.* 3200 BC) depicting two bulls back to back, one of which is being attacked by a lion. The bulla was shaped round the knot in a piece of two-strand string (of which the impression can be seen at one end). Excavated at Nineveh in northern Iraq. Length 6.0 cm. London, British Museum, WA 127389.

2B Neo-Assyrian clay bulla of the 7th century BC, excavated at Nineveh. It shows a king grasping a lion by its mane and stabbing it. This design, known as the 'royal seal type', occurs from the 9th century BC onwards in a variety of sizes, with differences in dress and border. It seems to have been the seal of the royal palace administration. This example is *c.* 2.4 cm in diameter and has a string-hole. London, British Museum, WA 84672.

3 Impression of a Middle Assyrian cylinder seal of the early 13th century BC on pottery, either as a mark of ownership or for decoration. Excavated at Tell Mohammed Arab in northern Iraq. Two goats leap up towards a tree on a hill; there are two birds in the tree, vegetation sprouts from the hill and a plant grows behind the goats. There are line borders above and below. Similar impressions occur on tablets from Ashur belonging to the reign Adad-nirari I (1305–1274 BC). Original seal *c.* 2.95 cm high and *c.* 1.2 cm in diameter. Baghdad, Iraq Museum, MA 455.

Early stamp seals

It is unlikely that the earliest stamps were intended for use on clay since no clay sealings from the early period have survived. Some of the earliest stamps date to the seventh and sixth millennia BC and come from the sites of Buqras in Syria, where they are made of stone, and Çatal Hüyük in central Turkey, where they are made of baked clay. They have a knob on the back and are circular, oval or cruciform. They may have been used for stamping textiles, leather, skin or even bread. Some of the earliest stone stamps were cut with simple linear designs (fig. 1A) that resemble those on the bread stamps still used in certain parts of the world. Similar linear designs are also found on early amulets but again without any evidence of sealing. The first clay sealings appear in the late fifth millennium BC at sites such as Değirmentepe in Turkey and Tepe Gawra and Nineveh (fig. 4) in northern Iraq. Actual stone seals of this period, pierced with a hole so that they could be worn, have also been found. They bear designs which include animals and humans and they immediately precede the invention of writing.

Writing and cylinder seals

Southern Mesopotamia has few natural resources but irrigation agriculture makes it fertile. The development of irrigation involved a high degree of co-operation and organisation; resources were pooled and surplus produce could be exchanged for the raw materials lacking in the alluvial south but available

4 Drawing of a Prehistoric stamp seal of the mid 4th millennium BC, reconstructed from six fragmentary impressions on clay sealings excavated at Nineveh in northern Iraq. The reverse of one of these indicates that it was impressed on a basket. The seal depicted dogs resembling modern salukis with cropped ears. The dents at the top and bottom show that the perforation through the seal had become worn – presumably because the seal was threaded onto a string. The largest impression on the photograph measures 3.15 × 3.05 × 1.0 cm. London, British Museum, WA 124342, 124344, 124347 and 138459.

in the highland zones to the north and east. So trading expeditions were sent out along the rivers to obtain the metals, stone and wood that southern Mesopotamia lacked.

The first known administrative 'documents' associated with this trade consist of clay tokens which have been found at a number of sites throughout the Ancient Near East dating from the ninth millennium BC onwards. The tokens were variously shaped and marked to represent different commodities and numerals. By about 3500 BC there is evidence from Susa in south-western Iran for the tokens being enclosed in clay balls that were sealed (fig. 5) and would accompany a consignment to its destination; in the event of a dispute the contents could be checked by breaking the ball. It was found convenient to have a summary of the shapes and numbers of tokens indicated by impressed signs on the exterior of the clay ball and from there it was a short step to dispensing with the tokens altogether and flattening the ball into a more convenient tablet shape. This step seems to have been taken at Uruk in southern Mesopotamia and this early form of notation is the first writing.

In order to seal the clay balls and tablets a new form of seal was developed that could cover a large area more swiftly than the stamp seal. This was the cylinder seal (fig. 6) which, as its name implies, was a cylinder, generally of stone, that was carved with a design and rolled across the clay to leave a continuous repeating design. Early cylinders had a handle on top, sometimes shaped like an animal. By about 3000 BC cylinder seals were generally perforated longitudinally so that they could be worn round the owner's neck or wrist, or suspended from a pin that fastened the garment. The cylinder seal was particularly adapted to use in Mesopotamia, where clay for making tablets was plentiful and where a system of writing rapidly developed that consisted in impressing wedge-shaped signs into clay with a stylus.

5 Clay ball bearing the multiple impressions of two cylinder seals of the Uruk period (c. 3400 BC), excavated at Susa in south-western Iran. One seal depicts five naked, bearded prisoners with their hands tied behind their backs, facing left; one of the prisoners is smaller than the others, and below him is a small animal facing right. The other seal shows a boar and a goat facing right. The ball contained clay tokens and was an early administrative document; it is 7.2 cm in diameter. Paris, Louvre Museum, AO Sb 4852 (F 606).

6 An Old Babylonian cylinder seal of the 18th century BC, rolled out to leave a modern impression. A kilted warrior king stands holding a mace before the interceding goddess Lama; behind the king stands a figure on a dais (perhaps a cult statue), holding an animal offering and wearing a square-topped head-dress, and behind Lama is a seated god holding a rod and ring – symbols of divinity; the crossed wedges above may depict a fly. The different styles of cutting of the robes of the goddess and seated god indicate that two different craftsmen were involved. Inscribed in cuneiform: *Ibni-Amurru, son of Ilima-ahi, servant of the god Amurru*. Haematite; 2.7 × 1.5 cm. London, British Museum, WA 89002.

This system of writing is known as cuneiform (from the Latin *cuneus*, a wedge) and its use spread to other areas of the Near East in response to the demands of trade. Originally it was used for writing the language of the inhabitants of southern Mesopotamia, the Sumerians. Later it was adapted for writing Akkadian – a Semitic language which developed into Assyrian in the north and Babylonian in the south of Mesopotamia. Cuneiform was also adapted for writing other Semitic languages and dialects and for writing totally unrelated languages such as Hurrian in Syria, Hittite and Urartian in Anatolia, and Elamite and Old Persian in Iran. It was deciphered in the first half of the nineteenth century and we can therefore read the languages written in cuneiform, many of which can be understood and translated thanks to the existence of bilingual and lexical texts.

The development of writing in Mesopotamia inspired the invention of independent systems, often better adapted to writing materials other than clay; for instance, the Egyptians and Hittites developed hieroglyphic scripts. As far as the archaeologist is concerned, the great advantage of dried clay is that it is far more durable than wood, leather or papyrus, and somewhere in the region of five hundred thousand tablets have already been found; many of these documents bear the impressions of seals.

The development of stamps and cylinders

The seals in the Ancient Near East were predominantly the stamp seal and the cylinder seal. The stamp seal was used in early, illiterate societies. It went on being used, after the development of writing, in societies that used writing materials other than clay and therefore only sealed the small clay bullae which were attached to goods or letters. Cylinder seals, as we have seen, were more suitable for sealing large areas on tablets or their clay envelopes, and on the large clay sealings of jars, containers and doors. Their use spread with the use of cuneiform and those countries which adopted the Mesopotamian cuneiform script also took over and adapted the cylinder seal. In some areas where cuneiform on clay and another script on a different material were current at the same period, a compromise seal was developed which was cylinder-shaped but also had a design carved on its base so that it could be used as a stamp seal. This form of seal is known as a stamp-cylinder (fig. 7).

Cylinder seals were used for over three thousand years. They ceased to be used when cuneiform writing on clay tablets was replaced by alphabetic scripts on other materials. Trade was once again the main impetus for the change. The countries along the eastern Mediterranean seaboard had long relied on trade for their livelihood. Their ships went to Egypt, Anatolia, Cyprus and the Aegean, and their caravans went eastwards to Mesopotamia and beyond. They had to make out their bills of lading in a variety of different languages written in scripts that had, as their only common denominator, the fact that they all consisted of several hundred different signs. An alphabet consists of no more than thirty signs and there were various attempts at inventing alphabets in the Levant during the second millennium BC. In the first millennium BC, the Phoenicians spread the use of the alphabet that bears their name; most modern ones are based on it. Gradually other administrations adopted its use

7 Stamp-cylinder, and its modern impressions, from the kingdom of Urartu in eastern Turkey (7th century BC). Three two-legged, winged, scorpion-tailed monsters stand on either side of a vertical fish; there are astral symbols and drill-holes in the field, and line borders top and bottom. The design on the base shows a similar bird-headed monster with astral symbols. Black stone; 2.95 (with loop) × 1.4–1.6 cm. London, British Museum, WA 130670.

and, concurrently, the use of the stamp seal. By the time of the fall of the Achaemenid Persian empire in 331 BC, cuneiform had ceased to be used in the administration and the cylinder seal was obsolete.

The Greeks, and later the Romans, adopted the alphabet and the stamp seal, and produced a series of miniature works of art generally referred to as *gems* because many of them were cut in semi-precious stones. Although a number of these gems were found within the geographical limits set out above, they do not belong to Ancient Near Eastern glyptic, whose traditions survived in the seals of the Parthians (250 BC–AD 224) and in the far more numerous seals of the Sasanians (AD 224–651). The advent of Islam in the seventh century AD led to the adoption of a new style of non-representational glyptic which was not restricted to the Near East and is outside the scope of this book.

Stamp versus cylinder

Seals
For the purposes of interpreting the past, cylinder seals provide far more information than stamp seals. There are a number of reasons for this. Stamp seals, as we have seen, were most closely associated with illiterate cultures or cultures that used perishable writing materials. As a result the administrative context in which stamp seals were used is frequently missing. The illiterate cultures were generally poorer or technically less advanced, so their seals were often made of soft, easily available stones and showed little variation in design from period to period. Stamp seals are generally classified according to changes in shape, but there was much conservatism with the same shape continuing in use for centuries. The surface that bears the design is smaller on a stamp seal

8   Cylinder seal, its ancient clay sealing and modern impression, excavated at Tell Asmar, ancient Eshnunna, in the Diyala region of central Iraq. The interceding goddess Lama, a male worshipper and a diminutive goddess stand before the god Tishpak, who has dragons' heads rising from his shoulders and is seated on a dais. Inscribed in cuneiform: *Tishpak, mighty king, king of the land of Warum: Kirikiri, governor of* *Eshnunna, to Bilalama, his son, has presented* *[this seal]*. Kirikiri probably ruled *c.* 2000 BC. This is one of the rare cases where both the ancient impression and the seal that made it have survived (see also figs. **11** and **26**). Lapis lazuli on a bronze or copper pin, with one gold cap surviving; 2.8 × 1.5 cm. Oriental Institute Museum, University of Chicago, A 7468.

than on a cylinder seal and leaves little space for an inscription. Such pieces as are inscribed generally have brief inscriptions – frequently only a name or title.

The design area on a cylinder seal is larger than that on a stamp seal and it has a direction. Miniature reliefs could be constructed; as the seal is rolled out these form either a continuous interlocking frieze or one which has clear-cut vertical divisions. The designs are more dynamic and elaborate than on most stamp seals. Cylinder seals were used by kings and highly placed officials and they reflect changes in fashion to a far greater degree than stamp seals. This is not only apparent in the types of designs used but also in the content: changes in dress, for instance, can be closely followed from one period to another and from one area to another. The materials and shapes of seals also change according to fashion and reflect variations in trade patterns. Since cylinder seals were used almost exclusively by literate administrations, they frequently bear long and informative inscriptions (fig. **8**).

The actual seals are often very attractive, regarded by their owners as pieces of jewellery that reflected their position and prestige. They were frequently kept as heirlooms and can be found in contexts that are much later than the period when they were made. As a result they are of less use for dating than sealings. Even sealings can be misleading at times because they could be made by a seal that was several generations old – sometimes one being used by a ruler as a dynastic seal to legitimise his claim to the throne. Seal designs or inscriptions were also often recut by later owners and it can be a tantalising puzzle to unravel the various stages of re-use in a seal's design (fig. **17**).

Sealings
The objects on which cylinder seals were impressed are generally larger than those on which stamp seals occur and they are therefore more easily found in archaeological excavations (compare figs. **2B** and **8**). Many sealings bear on their backs the impression of the object sealed and it is possible to identify the type of container, the material of which it was made (such as textiles, cane (fig. **4**), rushes or wood), and the locking device or rope that secured it. Sealings occur also on clay tablets which were often baked and which have survived better than unbaked bullae. The tablets on which they appear can generally be closely dated by content, script and language. Since tablets were far more often sealed with cylinders than stamps, it has been far easier to chronicle the changes in cylinder seals than in stamp seals. Furthermore, the administrative use of cylinder seals can be studied: we often know who used a cylinder seal, for what type of transaction and at precisely what date.

By their very nature sealings are usually fragmentary; they had to be broken so that the objects they sealed could be opened. They are therefore often found on the floors of storerooms, in rubbish tips or even re-used to level the floor of a later building. Generally the context of the sealings dates the period of use of a seal fairly accurately. Sometimes a seal was so often impressed, either on bullae, sealings or tablets or all three, that the whole of its design can be reconstructed from the evidence of numerous fragments. This is best done in a composite drawing (fig. **4**) since bullae are peculiar shapes and the design is frequently distorted. Surprisingly, among the many thousands of actual seals that have survived, there are only a handful for which we have been able to identify the ancient impressions (figs. **8, 11** and **26**).

Modern impressions

As seals were designed to be impressed on clay, their designs are best studied from impressions. It is usual, therefore, to make impressions of seals in clay, plaster or – more often nowadays – in one of the numerous modelling doughs or plasticines available. A medium that can be baked is the most convenient, as this makes the impression easier to handle. Most of the seal designs in this book have been illustrated by their modern impressions, generally much enlarged so that the details are apparent. The design on the impression is, of course, the reverse of what it was on the seal, but the descriptions in this book are of the designs as they appear on the impressions, usually beginning at the left. The sizes of the actual seals are given in the captions as height followed by diameter or, where relevant, as length, width and thickness.

— 2 —

Seals, the Antiquarian and the Archaeologist

The fifth millennium BC stamp seals of the Ancient Near East were the first in a long series. From then on seals were a mark of authority or prestige, and because they were used to protect property they acquired amuletic and talismanic protective benefits for their owner. Although some seals remained purely utilitarian, others became items of jewellery, were carved from rare or semi-precious stones (see ch. 3) and were sometimes set in gold (figs. **8** and **24**c). In Roman times gemstones became a popular material and were used to make seals known as gems. In medieval times documents were sealed with large 'seals' (we would call them bullae or sealings) hanging from ribbons and cast in a metal matrix (the equivalent to our seal). A papal 'bull' or edict was so named because of the bullae attached to it. With the revival of interest in Greek and Roman art during the Renaissance, gems were assiduously collected and just as assiduously copied. This interest continued and many large collections or 'cabinets' of gems were initiated during the next centuries.

Antiquarian interest

It is not certain when the first seal from the Ancient Near East entered a European collection. One very worn Akkadian seal from Mesopotamia, of about 2300 BC, was found among a group of stones said to have come from Golgotha, the site of Christ's crucifixion; they were brought back from the Holy Land by Crusaders and had been locked in a small reliquary in the Cappella Palatina in Palermo, Sicily. A Neo-Babylonian stamp seal of the sixth century BC and what were probably two recut Near Eastern stamp seals were illustrated in Francesco Bianchini Veronese's *La Istoria Universale* in 1697. A Neo-Babylonian and a Neo-Assyrian stamp seal are catalogued in Jacob de Wilde's *Gemmae selectae antiquae* (Amsterdam, 1703). Count Tubière de Grimoard de Caylus published his *Recueil d'antiquités égyptiennes, étrusques et romaines* in Paris in 1752 and included two cylinders seals from his collection which are now in the Bibliothèque Nationale in Paris; he ascribed both to the Persians and maintained that they had been found in Egypt. William Hamilton, a famous British collector of Greek vases and other antiquities, also had some cylinder seals, including one said to have been found at Marathon in Greece. He sold his collection to the British Museum in 1772.

Britain's involvement in India led to increased interest in the East. When in 1798 Napoleon invaded Egypt, the short route to India via Alexandria and the Red Sea was cut off, leaving, as alternatives, the long sea route round Africa or an overland route between the Mediterranean and the Gulf. The East India Company appointed a Resident in Baghdad named Claudius James Rich (1786–1821). Rich was a remarkable young man and in addition to being an excellent linguist he showed a keen interest in antiquities and travelled extensively throughout Mesopotamia. He assembled a large collection of manuscripts, coins, Assyrian and Babylonian antiquities, gems and seals. His collection was acquired by the British Museum in 1825. Subsequently expeditions of cartographers and engineers were sent to map the overland route and to investigate the possibility of navigation down the Euphrates or Tigris. Other enterprising young men extended their traditional Grand Tour to include not only Italy but Greece and the Ottoman Empire. They too brought back antiquities, among them several seals, which had the advantage of being both attractive and easy to carry.

Archaeological excavation

British interest in the Near East was matched by that of the French who, in 1842, established Paul-Emile Botta (1802–70) as Consul at Mosul on the Tigris in northern Mesopotamia. Botta immediately began the first archaeological excavations at Nineveh on the opposite bank of the river and also investigated another Assyrian capital nearby at Khorsabad. In 1845 the Englishman Austen Henry Layard (1817–94) also began digging at Nimrud and Nineveh. Since then archaeological work in Mesopotamia has been almost continuous. Layard's assistant Hormuzd Rassam (1826–1910) excavated at a number of sites, not only in the north but also in southern Mesopotamia. The Germans instituted excavations at Ashur in the north and at Babylon in the south. The Louvre in Paris, the British Museum in London and the Pergamon Museum in East Berlin, respectively, benefited considerably from the results of these nineteenth-century archaeological activities. For the first time provenanced seals entered Western collections (fig. 9).

A characteristic of Near Eastern archaeological sites is that many of them are *tells*. A tell is a mound, sometimes of considerable size, consisting of the superimposed ruins of ancient settlements. Tells are generally situated near a water course and often at a strategic point, such as a ford or crossroads. In the Near East, and particularly in Mesopotamia, mud bricks are the most common building material. Because wood is scarce, bricks are rarely fired except for use in the outer walls of an important religious or administrative building. As a result walls have to be plastered to protect them against weathering. When a building is abandoned, the wooden roof beams, door lintels and window frames are removed for re-use and the building rapidly collapses. Generally the upper walls are pulled down and the site is levelled to form a terrace that incorporates the lower part of the destroyed building; on this terrace the new building is constructed. Over the years the accumulation of superimposed buildings forms a mound which provides some kind of defence and protection from flooding; new houses therefore tend to be built on top of the mound but some

9 Modern impression of a cylinder seal obtained by Austen Henry Layard at Hillah near Babylon, in Iraq, before 1852. It is inscribed: *Ubil-Eshtar, brother of the king: Kalki, the scribe, is your servant.* Ubil-Eshtar, the prince, is the central figure of the composition and the focus of attention; he may have been a brother of Sargon of Akkad (2334–2279 BC), founder of the Akkadian dynasty. He carries an axe, as do two officers who wear the same type of wool robe. The man behind the prince is, presumably, Kalki the scribe, who is shown holding a small tablet in his left hand. It is possible that we have here the depiction of a highlight in Kalki's career, when he accompanied the prince on a foreign expedition from which he may have brought back the exotic black-and-white speckled stone (*see* **cover illustration**) from which his seal was carved. Indeed, the foremost figure in the scene is a mountain guide who is depicted wearing an unusual type of kilt and boots with upturned toes; he carries an early example of a short composite bow, an arrow and a quiver from which hangs a wool tassel for cleaning arrows (also shown on fig. **32**). Beneath the inscription, two servants carry camp furniture and provisions. Diorite; 3.32 × 2.05 cm. London, British Museum, WA 89137.

are terraced into its slopes. Eventually the mound becomes too steep and the space at its top so small that a new settlement is founded at its foot and grows up against it; alternatively the site can be shifted a few hundred metres away or even abandoned completely for this or other reasons. Although the advent of concrete as a building material has slowed the process, mounds are still being formed, particularly in rural areas.

When an archaeologist selects a mound for excavation, he or she examines the debris on the surface in order to establish the date of its latest occupation. Sherds of pottery are particularly useful in this respect because fashions in pottery change; gullies in the side of a mound will often provide a vertical section through the various levels and indicate at what periods the tell was occupied. The topmost levels will be the most recent and everything below will be earlier, although there may be gaps of several millennia in the sequence. Later houses terraced into the side of a mound or built up against it can, however, distort the picture and the untangling of the *stratification* of a mound is a complicated process.

Seals from excavations

In ancient Mesopotamia, and in many other areas of the Ancient Near East at different periods, the dead were buried under the floors of their houses.

23

These burials would be sealed in by later building activity and many tombs are found intact. They are accompanied by the personal belongings of the deceased, which vary according to status but rarely include spectacularly rich grave goods; however, they frequently include some beads and a cylinder seal. Care has to be taken to establish exactly the level from which a burial was dug in order to determine its date. As mentioned in chapter 1, however, seals are not as useful for dating a context as might at first appear. They were often kept as heirlooms and may have been buried in a much later grave. Furthermore, stone seals can roll down animal burrows and drains or drop into the bottom of a trench from a higher level and may therefore appear in a considerably earlier context than might be expected. Sometimes hoards of seals are discovered in temples; these are often of widely varying dates since they may have been dedicated to a deity over a long period of time. A comparable diversity of objects can be found today in our cathedral treasuries.

Sealings from excavations
Sealings were purely functional and were discarded after use. Many are found in rubbish tips. It is interesting, however, that there is far more evidence for sealings at some periods than at others. Rubbish tips containing large quantities of sealings have been found at several sites of the first half of the third millennium BC: Nineveh, Abu Salabikh, Fara and Ur (fig. **12**). In later periods greater use was made of seals for sealing tablets and their envelopes; these were stored in archives which often survive intact. There are large numbers of stamp seal impressions from the Assyrian palaces at Nineveh (eighth to seventh centuries

10 Some examples from a collection of 200 pieces of clay, impressed with coins and seals in a variety of styles. They were found in a grave of the Achaemenid Persian period (after 450 BC) at Ur in southern Iraq, and may have belonged to a jeweller or gem-cutter. The pointed ends of some of the seals indicate that they were ring-bezels. The second and fifth impressions in the top row show a hero, possibly Herakles, strangling a lion; the third shows the Mesopotamian heroes Gilgamesh and Enkidu beheading the giant Humbaba. The first seal impression in the bottom row was made by a gem depicting a Greek winged Victory; the second shows a priest on a Neo-Babylonian cylinder seal of the 6th century BC, the third and fourth were made by Achaemenid cylinder and conoid seals; the fifth depicts a deity on an Assyrian cylinder of the 8th century BC. The Achaemenid cylinder was 2.2 cm high. The collection was divided between the Iraq Museum in Baghdad, the British Museum in London and the University Museum in Philadelphia.

24

BC; fig. 2B), and archives of the Achaemenid Persian period (fifth century BC) contain many sealed bullae. A grave at Ur, dating to after 450 BC, contained two hundred impressions of Assyrian, Babylonian, Egyptian, Achaemenid Persian, Greek and Phoenician seals (fig. 10), and of some coins and metalwork. These were on small pieces of clay which had been baked to preserve them. It is thought that they may have belonged to a gem-cutter or jeweller who wished to keep a record of his own and other craftsmen's work.

Although sealings are generally discarded shortly after use and are therefore more useful for dating a context, they are not always an indication of local seal styles. Indeed, the sealings frequently arrived on bales or crates of merchandise from another town or even from abroad. In recent years an attempt has been made to establish, by studying their backs, which sealings were impressed locally and which were on imported goods. It has been demonstrated that some sealings were moulded around pegs in order to seal storerooms and presumably these would have been impressed with the seals of local officials. The backs of these sealings show the flat, grainy surface of the wooden door on one face, and the shape of the peg, wrapped around with string, that was used to secure the door. At Mari on the Middle Euphrates in Syria, in the 1760s BC, the storerooms were frequently sealed by an individual named Ana-Sin-taklaku, whose seal was later recut. It was acquired in the 1960s in Teheran (fig. 11). This is one of the rare examples where the ancient impressions of a surviving seal are known.

11   Modern impression of a cylinder seal originally belonging to *Ana-Sin-taklaku, son of Darish-libur, servant of Zimri-Lim* (king of Mari up to *c.* 1760 BC). The seal is known from many impressions of it on sealings found during excavations at Mari. Later in the 18th century BC, the inscription was recut by a new owner, *Adad-sharrum, son of Shamaiatum, servant of the god Ninshubur*. The actual seal depicts a goddess, whose dress falls open to reveal her nudity; the interceding goddess Lama; and a warrior god trampling an enemy underfoot. Facing these deities is a bearded king who holds a mountain goat as an animal offering; in the field are a rosette representing the sun, a recumbent gazelle and a goose. Haematite; 2.7 × 1.5 cm. Paris, Louvre Museum, AO 21988.

Sealings on imported merchandise also provide much interesting information, which is still in the process of being sifted and analysed. There must, for instance, be some significance in the fact that the backs of so many sealings of the early third millennium BC from northern Syria and northern Mesopotamia bear the impressions of baskets (fig. 4). This is rarely found elsewhere and may illustrate a preference for transporting or storing goods in baskets. A couple of unusual seal impressions from Ur, which probably date to the same period, bear impressions that must have been made by a seal that was almost identical to a fragmentary cylinder seal from Shahr-i Sokhta in eastern Iran (fig. 12). It is likely that these can be interpreted as evidence of trade between the two areas.

From about 1920 BC, for just under two centuries, the town of Ashur in northern Mesopotamia sent its merchants on trading expeditions to central Turkey. The merchants carried tin and textiles which they exchanged for gold and silver. Archives of tablets have been found in the merchant colony at Kanesh (modern Kültepe, just north of Kayseri). The clay envelopes of these tablets were sealed by seals in a variety of styles (fig. 13), including an elaborate local Anatolian style with minute designs carved on small seals made of very hard stones such as haematite. Further west, at the site of Acemhöyük, the local Anatolian palaces contained storerooms full of broken bullae. Some of these bullae had been sealed by Anatolian stamp seals, but others bore the impressions of cylinder seals of a sister of King Zimri-Lim of Mari on the Euphrates, of King Shamshi-Adad of Assyria, who carved out a huge north Mesopotamian kingdom between 1809 and 1776 BC, and of servants of King Aplahanda of Carchemish on the Syrian–Turkish border.

We have little evidence as to where the Assyrians obtained their tin. The documentation for that part of the trade is missing, but it seems clear that it came from the east. Recently tin has been found to the north of Afghanistan and Soviet excavations east of the Caspian have shown that at about this time the stamp-cylinder was adopted as a seal type. This, as we have seen in chapter 1, is always an indication of trade contacts with Mesopotamia. Furthermore, seal impressions on pottery from the site of Taip-Depe in that area are in a style that was clearly influenced by contemporary Syrian seals. These finds are the only evidence so far for the eastern part of the trade route which brought tin to Anatolia in the early centuries of the second millennium BC.

'Discrepancies' in the archaeological record
Some seal impressions are tantalising in that they are the only evidence for categories of seals which have not survived. Does this mean that the seals

12 Drawing of a seal impression on clay sealings of the early 3rd millennium BC, excavated at Ur in southern Iraq. An almost identical design appears on a fragmentary seal excavated at Shahr-i Sokhta in eastern Iran, near the Afghan border. This is some 1300 km from Ur as the crow flies and illustrates the vast distances covered by merchants. The seals were originally c. 3.5 cm high. The impressions are in the British Museum in London, U 14143, 14787; the seal is in Teheran, Iran Bastam Museum.

13 Clay envelope encasing a tablet, dating to the period between *c.* 1920 and 1850 BC when an Assyrian trading colony flourished at Kanesh (modern Kültepe in central Turkey). This envelope is sealed by an Assyrian merchant (bottom seal) and his Anatolian counterpart (top seal) and illustrates how the Mesopotamian iconography of fig. **33** was adapted in outlying regions. Every available space on the Anatolian seal has been filled, which is typical of Anatolian seals generally. Height of envelope 5.8 cm. London, British Museum, WA 113583A.

were made of perishable materials? Or that the goods were sealed in a remote area which has not, so far, been investigated? Or that the seals were buried with their owners and have not so far been found? The sealings of the third quarter of the second millennium BC from the Mitannian site of Nuzi in northern Mesopotamia are problematic. Excavations there uncovered a number of business archives with tablets sealed by well over two thousand different seals. Some of the tablets bore the impressions of relatively simple Common Style Mitannian seals similar to the seal illustrated on figure **14**, while others, possibly rather later in date, had designs which, by contrast, were in what is known as an Elaborate Style. Many hundreds of Common Style seals have survived all over the Ancient Near East – as far west as Mycenae in Greece and Vélez-Málaga in Spain, as far east as Marlik near the Caspian in Iran and as far south as the island of Failaka in the Gulf. They are made of faience (a term used, in the Ancient Near Eastern field, to describe a composite glazed material) which has often weathered badly. We know from the few Elaborate Style seals

14 Modern impression of a cylinder seal excavated at Tell Atchana (Turkey) and probably dating to between 1400 and 1350 BC. It shows two male figures standing on either side of a stylised tree; two couchant antelopes are set at right angles to the field between two different types of running spiral decoration. There are line borders at the top and bottom of the seal. Faience; 2.7 × 1.25 cm. London, British Museum, WA 130649.

that have survived, and from the high quality of the impressions, that the seals were finely carved out of stone. Why have so few of these high quality seals survived when so many of the more friable ones have? We cannot, at present, answer this question.

Although Nuzi provides an extreme example, it is a fact that the actual seals found in the excavations on a site rarely correspond in type to the impressions from the same site. I have made a careful study of both the impressions and the seals from the site of Tell Atchana on the Syrian–Turkish border. This mound was excavated by the English archaeologist Leonard Woolley (1880–1960) immediately before and after the Second World War. Two archives of tablets, dated respectively to Level VII (c. 1720–1625 BC) and Level IV (fifteenth century BC, contemporary with the earlier part of Mitannian Nuzi), established the identity of the site with the ancient city of Alalakh and showed that it was part of the Kingdom of Iamhad – the ancient name for Aleppo. Many of the envelopes from Level VII were sealed with seals of the kings of Iamhad (fig. **15**) and their brothers or cousins, the governors of Alalakh. The actual seals found in burials on the site were generally of much poorer quality. Either the tombs of the governors and high officials have not so far been found, or they were located in the vicinity of Aleppo. We may have, at Alalakh, copies of the royal correspondence which related to the site and which had been sealed by the king and his officials either in Aleppo or during royal visits to Alalakh. About sixty Mitannian seals were found at Alalakh, mostly belonging to the Common Style (fig. **14**); eighteen were found in Level IV, but there were only two impressions of (different) Common Style seals on the tablets from that level. Most of the other Common Style seals were found in later levels.

Glyptic as evidence of trade

The widespread occurrence of Mitannian Common Style seals, referred to above, illustrates another important aspect of seals: their distribution is evidence

15 Fragmentary clay envelope excavated in the ruins of the Level VII palace of ancient Alalakh (Tell Atchana in Turkey). It bears the impression of the seals of ten witnesses to a legal case concerning the division of property. The seal on the right in the photograph belonged, according to the cuneiform inscription, to *Niqmepuh, son of Iarim-Lim, king of Iamhad, servant of the god . . . .* Iamhad was the ancient name of Aleppo in northern Syria and Alalakh seems to have been one of the country palaces of the kings of Aleppo. On the seal the king receives the Egyptian *ankh* – symbol of life – from a Syrian goddess; the Mesopotamian interceding goddess Lama stands behind. The king and the Syrian goddess wear robes with thick borders (perhaps fur) and distinctive tall head-dresses. The head-dresses of both goddesses are horned to denote divinity. London, British Museum, WA 131449A.

of contacts between various areas of the Ancient Near East and beyond at a given time. The Common Style seals were mass-produced in various workshops and it is possible to trace the diffusion of groups of seals over a wide area. Seals from a workshop on the north Syrian coast at Ugarit have been found at Ugarit itself (about a dozen), Idalion and Enkomi on Cyprus, Tell Mohammed Arab in northern Iraq and Hasanlu in north-west Iran. Products of another workshop, possibly situated in or near Hazor north of Galilee, have been found at Hazor, Dhekelia on Cyprus, Kamid el Loz in the Lebanon, and Ashur and Tell Mohammed Arab in northern Iraq.

16 Modern impression of a Neo-Assyrian cylinder seal of the 8th century BC, excavated in the sanctuary of the Greek goddess Hera on the island of Samos, off the west coast of Turkey. The design shows a bearded worshipper, presumably the owner of the seal, facing an armed god, possibly the storm god, who stands on a bull; behind the worshipper stands an armed goddess on a podium. In the field are a crescent moon, a rhomb (symbol of fertility), a fish, a wheel, seven drill-holes indicating the Pleiades, a winged sun-disc and a bird (?). There are line borders at the top and bottom of the seal. Blue chalcedony on bronze mount; 4.2 × 1.65 cm. Berlin, Antikenmuseum, Sa 206.

17 Modern impression of a cylinder seal found in the shipwreck at Ulu Burun near Kaş, off the south coast of Turkey. The seal was originally cut in the Old Babylonian period, probably in the second half of the 18th century BC. The design consisted of a warrior king and the interceding goddess Lama beneath a star-disc and crescent (see fig. 42), with the diminutive figure of a priest between them, and a three-line cuneiform inscription. Later the inscription was erased, but traces of the wedges and vertical frame-lines can still be seen beneath the figure of a lion-griffin, stars and rosettes that have been carved in its place. The style of the griffin places it in the reign of the Assyrian king Assur-uballit I (1363–1328 BC). The circles drilled with a tubular drill may also have been carved then, but the kilted figure holding a sickle-sword and raising one hand was probably cut a few years later, around 1300 BC. These recuttings may turn out to be crucial in the dating of the wreck. Haematite; 2.85 × 1.15–1.2 cm. Bodrum Museum, KW 881.

Temple treasures have already been mentioned because of the chronological variety of the material they contain. The objects frequently came from far-distant places. In the temple of the goddess Hera on the island of Samos, off the west coast of Turkey, a large collection of votive objects was found including two Neo-Assyrian cylinder seals of the eighth century BC (fig. 16). The Oxus Treasure, which may have originated in a temple of the goddess Anahita on the Oxus river just north of Afghanistan, contained numerous votive objects of gold, including ten gold signet rings, and three quartz seals – one stamp and two cylinders – of the sixth to fourth centuries BC (fig. 27).

Texts tell of seals sent as special gifts. A shipwreck is in course of excavation off the south coast of Turkey, at Ulu Burun near Kaş in Lycia. Several cylinder seals, an Egyptian gold scarab seal with the name of Queen Nefertiti and other seals have so far been found. One of the cylinders (fig. 17) is particularly interesting in that it had obviously been kept as an heirloom for several centuries and frequently been recut. Other examples of seals shipped to distant destinations will be discussed in chapter 3.

—— 3 ——

The Evidence of the Materials

A study of their materials and shapes indicates that the first stone seals were probably made from smooth river pebbles. The softer stones were preferred because they were simpler to cut (see ch. 4) but the range of materials available is somewhat limited: chlorites and limestones, often in dark colours. Sometimes there is evidence of a conscious use of brighter-coloured stones and this had clearly become a priority by the end of the fifth millennium BC. In Mesopotamia cliffs of conglomerate (for instance along the river Tigris above Eski Mosul and at Samarra) were used as a source not only then, but also almost three thousand years later for many Middle Assyrian and Kassite seals. There is evidence at Tepe Gawra in northern Mesopotamia of the search for exotic materials; in Level XIII (late fifth millennium BC), beads of 'white paste, carnelian, obsidian and limestone ... turquoise, amethyst, lapis lazuli, agate, quartz, jadeite, beryl, diorite, haematite, steatite and serpentine' were recorded. Stamp seals were also made of some of these materials.

The greatest variety in the types of stones used in any one period is probably to be found in Mesopotamia under the Akkadian dynasty (c. 2340–2200 BC). The many Akkadian cylinder seals are cut in a distinctive style; they are exceptionally large and of unusually high quality. Greenstone – a stone used only at this period and for some scarabs in the first millennium BC (fig. 24c and cover illustration) – was popular (fig. 32); so was shell – the core of large marine shells – recognisable by a spiral curl visible on the ends of the seal. Harder materials were also cut with equal success: there are red and green jasper seals and a number in rock-crystal. Two rock-crystal seals from Ur have their central perforations painted in alternating red and white stripes and the decoration is visible through the transparent stone. Black-and-white speckled diorite also occurs (fig. 9 and cover illustration); limestone, however, is not common. Given the preference for coloured and unusual stones, it is certain that if lapis lazuli had been readily available, it would have been used much more extensively than it was. By far the most common material, however, particularly during the earlier part of the period, was dark, blackish-green serpentine. Analysis of the seal stones in the British Museum shows that serpentine virtually disappeared at the end of this period and only reappeared in Assyria in the early

18 Modern impression of a Neo-Assyrian seal of about 700 BC showing the owner of the seal before the armed warrior goddess Ishtar, who stands on her lion; crossed rampant ibexes and a date-palm. In the field is an earring – perhaps a royal gift to a high-ranking official. There are line borders at the top and bottom of the seal. The seal cutting is of exceptionally high quality and the material of which the seal is made is extremely rare and may have been imported from Kashmir or the Urals (*see* **cover illustration**). Green (grosular) garnet; 4.3 × 1.8 cm. London, British Museum, WA 89769.

centuries of the first millennium BC. The seal cutters of the last two centuries of the third millennium used chlorite instead of serpentine. We do not know why there was this change of material. It is unlikely that it was due to a change in fashion, since the two stones look very much alike, although serpentine has a more waxy appearance. Was the source of serpentine (wherever it was) no longer accessible? Or, since chlorite is somewhat softer than serpentine, was the reason for the change purely one of convenience?

In the eighth century BC in Assyria, and probably somewhat earlier in Babylonia, quartz became the principal seal material, with a particular preference for two of its forms: blue chalcedonies and orangey-red cornelians. Seal analysis has shown, however, that two seals in the British Museum which were previously thought to be of green chalcedony are, in fact, green (grosular) garnet (fig. **18** and cover illustration). This is a most unusual material and since the main source – in South Africa – is out of the question, it seems likely that it came from Kashmir or the Urals. Purplish red (almandine) garnets became popular for Sasanian seals between the third and early seventh centuries AD. Although hard materials had been used from very early periods, they had only been adopted for exceptional seals. The change, in the first millennium BC, to a predominance of hard materials probably reflects improved techniques of stone cutting; these will be discussed in chapter 4.

Rare stones were always prized but there were definitely fashions in stones. This was due to availability and partly to the ease with which they could be worked or their suitability as seal stones. Turquoise, for instance, was hardly ever used because it is a very absorbent stone and would probably have become discoloured if rolled repeatedly over damp clay. It is worth looking at some seal stones in detail, as the evidence they yield is particularly significant.

Lapis lazuli

Lapis lazuli is a very attractive royal blue stone (see cover illustration). Its importance for archaeologists lies in the fact that it was only obtainable in antiquity from mines in the Badakhshan district of Afghanistan. (There is some evidence for another source near Quetta in Pakistan but its early use has not, so far, been established and it is in any case equally distant.) The presence of lapis lazuli in an archaeological context is therefore an indication of contact, whether direct or indirect, with Afghanistan.

At Tepe Gawra a lapis lazuli stamp seal was found, bearing a design similar to our figure 4 and probably to be dated to about 3600 BC, while a hemispheroid stamp seal made of lapis lazuli, with a design consisting of a standing figure, was found in a tomb dated a century or so later. In a hoard of the late fourth millennium BC from Uruk in the south, there were two lapis lazuli cylinder seals. A text records trade in lapis lazuli which Enmerkar, a king of Uruk in the early third millennium BC, received in exchange for grain from the people of Aratta, who were skilled craftsmen and 'brought down the stones of the mountains from their highland'.

The presence of lapis lazuli in Mesopotamia fluctuated considerably but it is certain that our view of the trade is distorted by the huge gaps in our knowledge. Were it not for the discovery of the Royal Cemetery of Ur by Leonard Woolley, the scale of the trade would be completely unknown to us (fig. 19). As it is, of the 1840 graves excavated, a sixth contained lapis lazuli objects, sometimes in impressive quantities. About 140 lapis lazuli cylinder seals from Ur can be dated to the Early Dynastic III period (c. 2600–2340 BC). Almost forty belong to the succeeding Akkadian period (c. 2340–2200 BC) but there are only a handful for the final two hundred years of the third millennium. It could be argued that this decline in the number of lapis lazuli seals is a reflection of the political decline of Ur in the Akkadian period, but this argument does not hold good for the last century of the third millennium when Ur was the dominant economic and political power in Mesopotamia. That the fall in the number of lapis lazuli cylinder seals reflects a hiatus in the trade is borne out by the fact that the Akkadian-period lapis lazuli seals from Ur account for more than half the known Akkadian seals in that material and the lapis lazuli is generally of much poorer quality.

At no other period do we have evidence for the import of such huge quantities of lapis lazuli as during the Early Dynastic III period. The material is also attested at other contemporary sites, particularly at Kish in central Mesopotamia and at Mari on the Middle Euphrates. Despite the subsequent reduction in the lapis lazuli trade, however, the stone remained extremely popular and was much in demand. Evidence for this comes in the form of two hoards.

The Tod treasure
Bronze boxes bearing the name of the pharaoh Ammenemes II (1929–1895 BC) were found buried in a temple at Tod, on the Nile near Thebes in Egypt. The treasure consisted of weights, ingots and jewellery of silver and gold – much

19 Modern impression of an Early Dynastic III cylinder seal found in a grave of c. 2600 BC in the Royal Cemetery at Ur, in southern Iraq. It is inscribed in cuneiform: *Pu-abi, queen*. The design is divided into two registers depicting banquet scenes involving the queen, possibly in her role as priestess, and her consort or a priest. Lapis lazuli; 4.9 × 2.5 cm. London, British Museum, WA 121544.

33

of it fragmentary – a silver and electrum container, several dozen silver vessels that had been flattened and folded, and a large amount of scrap lapis lazuli including fourteen cylinder seals and three stamp seals. Most of these seals were broken, chipped, worn or recut and had obviously not been kept for their aesthetic value. Lapis lazuli was used as inlay in jewellery, however, and the seals were probably treasured as a source of raw material. The style and designs of the seals show that they range in date from the first half of the third millennium BC to *c.* 1900 BC and were made in Iran, Mesopotamia and Syria.

The Thebes hoard

Towards the end of the nineteenth century some cuneiform tablets appeared on the market in Egypt. Their source was found to be Tell el-Amarna and more tablets were excavated at the site. It transpired that the Amarna Letters, as they are known, were the royal correspondence of pharaohs of the fourteenth century BC with the rulers of Babylonia and Assyria in Mesopotamia, Mitanni in northern Syria, the Hittites and Arzawa in Anatolia, and Cyprus, as well as endless letters from the governors of the petty semi-independent states along the Levant coast. They wrote in a dialect of Akkadian, which was then the *lingua franca* of diplomacy. The royal correspondence includes fascinating inventories of objects requested or sent as 'diplomatic gifts' – in fact a form of trade in prestige goods. Lapis lazuli features constantly as an item that the rulers of Mesopotamia sent in exchange for gold. In Letter 16 the Assyrian king Ashur-uballit I (1363–1328 BC) specifies that he is sending 'a seal in genuine lapis lazuli' for which he wants gold 'which, in your country, is dust – one only has to pick it up!'. Almost always lapis lazuli is qualified as 'genuine'. The reason for this was that blue glass was being manufactured as a substitute for lapis lazuli. Most of the surviving blue glass beads and seals have weathered so that they are white and only look blue where they are chipped. However, two seals of kings of Sidon, probably of the thirteenth century BC, are still perfect copies of lapis lazuli; they were catalogued as such in the last century and have only recently been identified as glass.

This trade in lapis lazuli is the background to the second hoard which was found in 1963 at Thebes in Greece in a Mycenaean level. It contained gold,

20 Modern impression of a cylinder seal from a hoard excavated at Thebes in Greece. It belonged to *Kidin-Marduk, son of Sha-ilimma-damqa, the 'sha-reshi' official of Burnaburiash, king of the world*. Burnaburiash II was a Kassite king of Babylonia from 1359–1333 BC. The seal depicts a god of fertility and water, who rises between two mountains on which grow flowers and trees; he holds two vases from which streams of water flow into two other vases. Lapis lazuli; 4.18 × 1.5 cm. Thebes Museum.

34

agate and lapis lazuli objects including thirty-six lapis lazuli cylinder seals. Many of the seals were either of Cypriote origin or had been recut in Cyprus. Others came from Babylonia, including one with the name of the Kassite king Burnaburiash II (1359–1333 BC) – one of the kings engaged in the Amarna correspondence (fig. 20). Not all the seals were as fine, however, and several had clearly been imported as scrap lapis lazuli for re-use. The Babylonian lapis lazuli weighed approximately one *mina* (c. 500 g) and may have been sent as a gift – perhaps by the Assyrian king Tukulti-Ninurta I (1243–1207 BC) after he had captured Babylon and, presumably, raided its temple and palace treasuries.

Later hoards
The temple treasuries of Babylonia were raided again in the sixth century BC by the Achaemenid Persians, in whose treasury in Persepolis a number of Babylonian votive seals were found. The seals were mostly of lapis lazuli and were fragmentary and burnt – presumably in the destruction of Persepolis by Alexander the Great in 331 BC. They must, however, have been exceptionally large and had been carved in relief, which is most unusual. The inscriptions tell us that some of the objects had been dedicated by Assyrian kings. Two similar votive seals were excavated in Babylon; one of them was of lapis lazuli (fig. 21).

Agate and cornelian

Other materials were imported from distant lands for the manufacture of seals. These included banded brown and white agate and orangey-red cornelian, which were probably obtained as beads from the west coast of India. There were large numbers of beads in these materials in the Royal Cemetery of Ur and they are generally barrel-shaped. It is perhaps for this reason that some seals in these materials are also barrel-shaped; barrel-shaped agate seals were particularly popular in the Achaemenid Persian period (sixth to fifth centuries BC).

21 Drawing of the design carved in relief (instead of the usual intaglio) on an exceptionally large Neo-Babylonian votive seal of the first half of the 1st millennium BC, excavated at Babylon in Iraq. The storm god Adad is shown with a lion-griffin on a leash, and holding forked lightning in both hands. The cylinder was engraved with inscriptions cut so as to be read on the cylinder, as was customary in the 1st millennium BC, although earlier seals were usually inscribed in reverse so as to be legible on the impression. The original inscription, perhaps of the 9th century BC, states that this was *The seal of the god Adad*; later two straddling lines were added to make it: *The property of the god Marduk . . . of Esagila* (Marduk's temple in Babylon). Later still the Assyrian king Esarhaddon (680–669 BC) added yet another inscription: *To the god Marduk, great lord, his lord, Esarhaddon, king of the universe, king of Assyria, has given [this seal] for his life.* Lapis lazuli; 12.5 × 3.2 cm. Berlin, Pergamon-museum.

22 Modern impression of a Syrian cylinder seal of the 18th century BC. The seal is typical of a workshop that produced high-quality seals made of exotic materials, especially – as here – green jasper. Motifs borrowed from Egypt are the hawks, monkey, sphinx with an elaborate plume-and-ram's-horns head-dress, falcon-headed Horus wearing the Egyptian double-crown and uraeus and holding a lotus, the kilted figure holding the *was* sceptre, and the scattered Egyptian hieroglyphs, some of which can be read as *hr*, contentment, and *rnr*, a personal name. The vertical guilloche and line borders are, however, typically Syrian, and the 'segmented style' of the birds and animals is characteristic of this workshop. Green jasper, or possibly greenstone; 2.0 × 1.0 cm. Ex-De Clercq Collection.

23 Drawing of the impression of a cylinder seal in the same style as seals of the 'green jasper' workshop (*see also* fig. 22). It, too, has motifs borrowed from Egypt, such as the hawks, lotus pattern, monkeys, sphinx in a plume-and-ram's-horns head-dress, trampling enemies, *ankh*, and figure with a curl of hair similar to that of the young Horus, holding a *was* sceptre. The vertical guilloche is typically Syrian and the 'segmented style' of the animals and birds is characteristic of the workshop. The cuneiform inscription enables some products of the workshop to be closely dated because the seal's owner, *Iaush-Addu, king of Buzuran,* is named on clay tablets of *c.* 1800 BC found at Mari, on the Euphrates in eastern Syria. Obsidian; 2.4 cm high. Jonathan P. Rosen Collection, New York.

Haematite

Although it is hard and difficult to cut, haematite is still a popular stone for signet rings because it produces a very sharp impression and is resistant to wear, although it does chip. It is a fine-grained grey stone with a metallic lustre and will take a high polish. It was used for almost all good quality seals during the first four centuries of the second millennium BC all over the Near East (fig. 6), but it was barely used before or after. Poorer quality seals were made of softer materials but these are often dark stones such as chlorite, serpentine and black limestones – presumably in cheaper imitation of haematite.

Green jasper

From about 1800 BC for at least two centuries one Syrian workshop was exceptional in that it produced high quality seals in materials other than haematite. It was probably situated somewhere in the neighbourhood of Byblos on the Lebanese coast and its seals were made from unusual materials with a marked preference for green jasper (fig. 22). Its products are distinguished by strong Egyptian influence (including the use of Egyptian hieroglyphs), by finely cut vertical guilloche patterns, and by a distinctive segmented representation of animals and birds (the bodies of the animals curve over the haunches, while the necks and bodies of the birds form a continuous line distinct from the wing). Products of this workshop were highly prized: the ruler of Buzuran near Mari on the Euphrates shortly after 1800 BC ordered an obsidian (volcanic glass) seal (fig. 23), and green jasper examples have been found as far afield as Cyprus, Crete and Carthage (in a tomb of the seventh or sixth century BC!). The green jasper probably came from Egypt, together with amethyst which was used for some seals and scarabs at this period. Many Phoenician scarabs of the first millennium BC are made of green jasper, although in some cases the term greenstone may be more accurate (fig. 24c).

Burnt steatite

Scarabs had originally been Egyptian amulets shaped like the scarab beetle – a symbol of the sun god. They became popular as seals and their use spread to Palestine (fig. 24A) during the first half of the second millennium BC. There was a revival in popularity of the scarab in the first millennium BC in Syria (fig. 24B–C), but whereas these scarabs were generally made of hard stones, the earlier scarabs (fig. 24A) were often made of steatite – a relatively softer soapstone – which was then burnt to form enstatite, which gave the seal a hard, pale coating. This technique seems to have been used at various periods, particularly for long thin cylinder seals decorated with geometric designs, found along a trade route between Susa in south-west Iran and Brak in Syria (fig. 25) and dating from the first centuries of the third millennium BC. The technique

24A Scarab seal, and its modern impression, excavated at Gezer in Palestine. Its inscription in Egyptian hieroglyphs indicates that it belonged to an Egyptian official of the Middle Kingdom (c. 2050–1786 BC): *The king's recorder, consort, Imeny, lord of honour.* Burnt steatite; 2.45 × 1.7 × 1.0 cm. London, British Museum, WA 104925.

24B Syrian Scarab seal and its modern impression. This seal belongs to a group known as the 'Yunus Cemetery Group' after the site near Carchemish on the Syrian–Turkish border where one example was found in a context dated to c. 700 BC. The design shows a winged sun-disc, two vultures, a lion and a bull with its head twisted between its legs. Haematite; 2.6 × 1.2 × 1.05 cm. London, British Museum, WA 103292.

24c Phoenician scarab seal of the 5th century BC, on an original gold swivel mount (*see* **cover illustration**), and its modern impression. It depicts a seated god. Greenstone ('green jasper'); 1.6 × 1.2 × 1.85 cm. London, British Museum, WA 136025.

25 Cylinder seal, and its modern impression, from Austen Henry Layard's expeditions in northern Mesopotamia between 1845 and 1851. The tall narrow shape, the material and the cruciform design are typical of the so-called 'Ninevite 5' style of the early centuries of the 3rd millennium BC. Burnt steatite; 5.0 × 1.1 cm. London, British Museum, WA 89843.

was also used for stamp seals of the late third and early second millennium BC on the islands of Failaka and Bahrein in the Gulf. These islands were staging posts in a trade between Mesopotamia and the Indus Valley, and 'Gulf' seals have also been found at various points along the trade-route (fig. 1c).

— 4 —

The Evidence of Technical Development

The development of stone-cutting techniques can be studied in great detail thanks to the vast body of material provided by seals, covering several thousand years. From 1978 onwards Len Gorelick and John Gwinnett, of the State University of New York at Stony Brook, published a series of articles, mainly in the American journal *Expedition*, on their pioneering work in establishing how the seals were cut. They used an electron miscroscope to examine the tool marks left by ancient seal cutters and discovered that each type of tool and abrasive leaves a distinctive mark. They set out to duplicate these ancient tool marks and thus establish which materials and abrasives were used at different periods.

Before 3000 BC

We saw in chapter 3 that the earliest seals were probably river pebbles, with a preference for those in soft stones. These were carved with very simple, linear designs relying on open-ended cuts created by running a flint tool backwards and forwards to form a groove (fig. 1A). The rate of cutting was accelerated by the use of an abrasive. Holes for suspension could be shaped by rotating a pointed flint. This technique was used for amulets at Arpachiyah in northern Mesopotamia in the Halaf period (late sixth millennium BC) but there is no evidence that the objects produced were used for sealing.

Flint tools were originally held in the fingers; later they were set in a wooden or bone handle which allowed for the application of more pressure and enabled the tool to be rotated between the palms of the hands, thus achieving greater speeds. Eventually the bow drill was developed: the string of a bow was wrapped around the tool and as the bow was pulled backwards and forwards, so the tool rotated. This greatly increased the speed of drills and 850 revolutions per minute could be achieved. Finally the bow drill was mounted horizontally so that, instead of vertical pressure being applied by the tool on the object being drilled, the object itself was held against the rotating drill. This led to far greater control and enabled curved surfaces – like those of a cylinder seal – to be cut. Indeed, horizontally-mounted bow drills are still used today by specialist craftsmen such as watch-makers or Indian bead-makers. By the end of the fourth millennium BC, therefore, designs could be more complex and, as discussed in chapter 3, the variety of stones being worked was impressive. A large number of coloured limestone stamp and cylinder seals bear designs of stylised animals made up of a series of drill-holes (fig. 1B). Perforations were drilled from each end to prevent overheating and splitting of the stone.

From about 3000 to 1500 BC

The next breakthrough is probably connected with a general switch from stone to copper tools. Copper tools may already have been used for cutting some hard stone Akkadian seals in court workshops in about 2250 BC, but with the advent of the second millennium BC, hard stones became the rule rather than the exception and haematite was ubiquitous. Although copper is a soft metal, a copper tool has the advantage of being soft enough for particles of abrasive to become embedded in the copper, and this makes it better suited for the cutting of stone than some harder materials. The modern equivalents are specially manufactured drills made from welding a mixture of powdered bronze or ceramic with diamond grits at a high temperature. With copper tools the abrasive is all-important, but fine abrasive – such as emery powder from the Cycladic island of Naxos in the Aegean – is an item of trade which, alas, has left little trace.

Although the drill was used for cutting the perforations and some designs, a large number of seals still bore linear designs which would have been cut with hand-held tools. In the second half of the eighteenth century BC, however, there seems to have been another technological breakthrough: the majority of seals from then on show the obvious use of the drill, together with the use of the cutting-wheel. This latter tool, also activated by a bow drill, enabled thick or thin cuts (depending on the thickness of the wheel) to be made in a seal's surface. Whole figures and scenes could therefore be constructed using drills and cutting-wheels of different sizes, and seals became mass-produced. It is possible that a more efficient method of powering the bow drill was also introduced at this time.

From about 1500 to 1200 BC

Synthetic materials led to mass-production of another type. Faience had probably been known since the fifth millennium BC, but the development of a glass industry towards the middle of the second millennium gave new impetus to its manufacture since the processes are related. Faience was used for the mass-production of cylinder seals with simple uninspired designs (fig. 14) which were traded over huge distances (see chapter 2). As a reaction to this mass-production there was an increase in the re-use of seals – heirlooms and dynastic seals (fig. 17) – and, from the fourteenth century BC, the search for unusual materials intensified. In Syria small cylinder seals of goethite (a material related to haematite), jasper, agate, cornelian and chalcedony were cut with cutting-wheels and drills of different sizes and with tubular drills. In Assyria beautiful, exciting new designs were carved in hard stones (figs. 3 and 26), and some of the more imaginative products from Kassite Babylonia are equally fine (fig. 20). Many of the stones used would seem to have been obtained locally from the cliffs of conglomerate along the Tigris. Glass cylinder seals are less well preserved

26 Modern impression of a Middle Assyrian cylinder seal of the early 13th century BC. It depicts a fallow deer nibbling at the lower branches of a tree. The horizontal cuneiform inscription informs us that this is the *Seal [of] Ashur-rimanni, son of Shumu-eṭir-Ashur*. This seal may have been used by Ashur-rimanni on a tablet now in Leiden but the impression is fragmentary; if so, this would be a rare example of the survival of both a seal and its ancient impression. Dark grey chalcedony; 2.8 × 1.2 cm. Paris, Bibliothèque Nationale.

but some, cut with cutting-wheel and drill, display a new freedom of composition incorporating such elements as animals, some of them mythical, pursuing each other.

From about 900 to 700 BC

Little is known about seal cutting in Mesopotamia during the dark age at the end of the second and beginning of the first millennium BC, and we are hampered by the lack of an adequate chronology. In the ninth century BC, possibly under Syrian influence, Assyria adopted a linear style on soft stones such as serpentine. Babylonia seems to have preserved or revived the cut-style animal designs of second-millennium glass seals and executed them in hard stones, especially cornelian. By the end of the ninth century BC Assyria had developed a cut-and-drilled style on chalcedony seals for representing deities (fig. **16**). A more carefully modelled style was adopted throughout Mesopotamia in the second half of the eighth century BC and beautiful cylinder seals were produced in various chalcedonies; there was a preference for cornelian, but some unusual materials such as green garnet (fig. **18** and cover illustration) are also represented. The style of cutting of these seals testifies to the existence of several workshops producing material of the highest quality. The continued use of hard stones from then on may indicate another technical innovation that made it easier to shape and cut these materials.

From about 700 to 250 BC

The shift to stamp seals, which took place at this time (figs. **1D** and **2B**), gradually led to a reduction in quality of execution. The many stylised Babylonian octagonal pyramidal seals of the sixth century BC (fig. **1D**) testify to the blight wrought by mass production. The stones themselves continued to be carefully shaped chalcedonies, with a preference for blue (see cover illustration). Contemporary cylinder seal designs were equally uninspired, with the exception of the products of a brief revival under the Achaemenid Persians in the sixth and fifth centuries BC (fig. **27**). Stamp seals were also used extensively in Syria during the first millennium BC. There are some beautiful haematite seals (fig. **24B**), and green jasper was also popular (fig. **24C**), with elaborate designs, often influenced by Egyptian motifs. Further south, quartzes were used extensively for oval seals (scaraboids) which generally bear simple, technically undemanding designs or, more often, brief alphabetic inscriptions.

27 Achaemenid Persian cylinder seal of the 5th century BC, and its modern impression. It formed part of the Oxus Treasure, which was probably the contents of a temple treasury, buried near the River Oxus (Amu Darya) in Turkmenistan. There are two scenes depicting a Persian warrior defeating a number of enemies while his god, Ahura-Mazda, looks on from a winged disc and crescent-disc. Chalcedony; 3.7 × 1.5 cm. London, British Museum, WA 124015.

From about 250 BC to AD 651

The scant surviving evidence for Parthian seals (*c.* 250 BC–AD 240) indicates strong Greek and Roman influence. Recent research has shown that diamonds were used for tools from about 250 BC onwards. The findings, based on material from a bead workshop at the site of Arikamedu in south-east India, give substance to the claim of the Roman author Pliny that diamond splinters were 'very much sought after by engravers of gems' in Roman times. Other texts refer to the use of engraved diamond and ruby seals by the Sasanian king Chosroes II Parviz (AD 591–628). The use of diamond tools would explain the increase in the number of seals of Roman and Sasanian date made of gemstones (fig. 1E).

Magnification

It should again be emphasised that most of the photographs in this book have been enlarged. The minute cutting of the finest seals has sometimes been used as an argument for the existence of lenses. In fact, craft workers who had the advantage of short-sightedness (myopia) would have been capable of producing even the most detailed designs without any form of optical aid. Crafts tend to be passed down from father to son and, since myopia is a dominant hereditary trait, it too would have been transmitted. Nevertheless, the skill with which these craftsmen executed their designs on recalcitrant stones with primitive tools is truly remarkable.

— 5 —

The Evidence of the Designs

The illustrations in this book provide some indication of the scope and variety of the designs on seals. In order to give coherence to a discussion of designs and iconography at different periods and in different areas of the Ancient Near East, I have limited myself here to one particular subject which was universally popular: the representation of deities.

The early periods

Early stamps bear geometric motifs. This may have been because of technical limitations, but it is also possible that there was a taboo involved in representing deities. The earliest depiction of a probable deity appears on stamp seals or their impressions of about 3400 BC from Susa in south-western Iran (fig. 28). Here the central figure in the composition seems to be the focus of worship and is shown in anthropomorphic form, although it is possible that the figure was animal-headed or wore a mask. Mesopotamia seems to have been slow to evolve a depiction of deities, although processions of figures approaching temples are shown in the latter part of the Uruk period (from *c.* 3300 BC), and symbols later associated with the goddess Inanna appear frequently (fig. 29).

The third millennium BC

During the Early Dynastic period (*c.* 2900–2350 BC) contest scenes, showing mythical heroes protecting animals from attack by predators, and banquet scenes

28 Stamp seal design reconstructed from impressions of the late 4th millennium BC, excavated at Susa in south-western Iran. It depicts a long-nosed (or masked?) figure, probably male, who wears an elaborate head-dress, a pendant and a long, patterned skirt, and raises a bowl. He is surrounded by figures presenting offerings. The seal was slightly convex and its diameter was *c.* 3.7 cm. Paris, Louvre Museum, Sb 2265–2267.

29 Modern impression of a cylinder seal of the Uruk Period (late 4th millennium BC) found near the site of Uruk in southern Iraq. It depicts a bearded male figure, generally referred to as the priest-king, who wears a thick band round his head and a net-patterned skirt. He holds two flowering branches which two leaping sheep are nibbling. At the end of the scene, two reed bundles with streamers – symbols of the goddess Inanna – frame a lamb above two tall ritual vessels. The bottom of the seal is badly broken; the top is decorated with a small figure of a recumbent lamb in copper – an early example of casting by the lost-wax method. Marble; 5.4 × 4.5 cm. Berlin, Pergamonmuseum, VA 10537.

(fig. 19) were popular. The participants in the banquets may represent deities, but it is more likely that they are priests, priestesses or rulers and their consorts. The earliest certain depictions of deities on seals belong to about 2400 BC, when figures wearing the horned head-dresses later associated with deities appear as objects of worship (fig. 30) or in mythological scenes. An extraordinary seal impression from Susa (fig. 31) shows an elaborate series of scenes arranged in two registers. Here animals serve to identify the deities: a hunting god stands on two dogs; a goddess kneels (in a pose characteristic of seals and sculptures from Iran generally) on two lions, and the wings or quivers rising from her shoulders relate her to winged warrior deities on Mesopotamian and Syrian seals (as for example in figure 32).

When Sargon of Akkad unified Mesopotamia under Akkadian rule in c. 2334 BC, he sought to give greater coherence to his kingdom by reorganising the religious pantheon and establishing a precise iconography for the various deities. The agricultural gods and goddesses of the Sumerians in the south were assimilated to the predominantly astral deities of the Semitic Akkadians. For instance, the goddess of fertility, Inanna, became merged with Ishtar, the goddess of love and war who was associated with the morning star (the planet Venus). The goddess in figure 32 is shown holding a bunch of dates, a symbol of fertility; weapons rise from her shoulders to indicate her warrior aspect, and she is winged to show that she is an astral deity. On later seals (fig. 34) she was also associated with a lion, but her warrior aspect continued to be stressed and she was a favourite patron of the warlike Assyrians (fig. 18). The sun god is also shown on figure 32; rays rise from him, and he ascends between the mountains of the east through which he has cut his way with a saw-toothed knife. On many other Akkadian seals he is seen with one foot placed on a mountain, still holding the knife; this aspect of his iconography was extremely popular in the Old Babylonian period, in the nineteenth and eighteenth centuries BC (fig. 35). The water god is also depicted on figure 32, where he is

30 Modern impression of an Early Dynastic cylinder seal (*c.* 2400 BC) which may have come from the site of Umma in southern Iraq. Two figures approach a bearded god who is seated on a throne supported by recumbent sheep; behind him is the façade of his temple and before him is an offering table on a bull-shaped stand. One of the approaching figures is probably a priestess and wears the thick headband later associated with the *en*-priestess; the other figure carries a spouted libation vessel. The god wears a horned tiara – an early use of such a head-dress to denote divinity; his identity is not known but he was probably a god of fertility or animal husbandry. Greenish translucent stone; 4.3 × 2.5 cm. Berlin, Pergamonmuseum, VA 3878.

31 Reconstructed drawing from impressions of a cylinder seal on jar sealings excavated at Susa in south-western Iran. The elaborate design, arranged in two registers, is unusual but the contest scene below, with a bull-man and hero stabbing one of two lions which are attacking a human-headed bull (probably a bison), is typical of the latter part of the Early Dynastic period (*c.* 2500 BC). This scene is flanked by two goddesses kneeling on lions: one faces a kneeling female worshipper, with a sun-disc, crescent and star between them, and the other is accompanied by two nude men holding branches. The upper register bears a fragmentary cuneiform inscription: *E-gi-...-dim, gold and pure silver*; in addition a hunting god stands on two dogs and holds a bow in the direction of a rampant goat; a goddess kneels on two lions, with weapons or wings rising from her shoulders; before her are a sun-disc, crescent and star, and a kilted worshipper with one hand raised; they are followed by a scorpion-man, a bird-demon, a monkey playing a flute, and a bull-headed figure stretching his arm towards a long-haired, kilted figure who holds a branch of vegetation. 3.75 cm high. Paris, Louvre Museum, S 462.

32 Akkadian cylinder seal (*c.* 2300 BC), and its modern impression, inscribed with the name of *Adda, scribe*. For a detailed discussion, see pp. 44–6. Greenstone; 3.9 × 2.4–2.55 cm (slightly concave). London, British Museum, WA 89115.

33 Cylinder seal (and its modern impression) found in Babylon in southern Iraq and dated by its cuneiform inscription to the reign of Ur-nammu, first king of the Third Dynasty of Ur (2112–2095 BC): *Ur-nammu, strong man, king of Ur: Hash-hamer, governor of Ishkun-Sin, is your servant.* An interceding and a leading goddess introduce the owner of the seal before the king, who wears the round, high-brimmed head-dress of royalty and sits on a bull-legged throne on a dais beneath a crescent moon. Greenstone; 5.28 × 3.03 cm. London, British Museum, WA 89126.

shown with streams of water flowing from his shoulders. He is frequently shown accompanied by nude attendants similar to that on the right in figure **42**. After the Akkadian period there are few depictions of him in Mesopotamia, but his popularity continued in outlying regions (fig. 37). In Mesopotamia his role seems to have been taken over by a deified mountain (fig. 20).

Another feature of figure **32** is the fact that its inscription identified the owner. Many early seals seem to have belonged to an administration dominated by the temple, rather than to a specific individual. Increasing secular power meant that during the second half of the Early Dynastic period inscriptions appear on seals, naming the owner and indicating that they were personal seals. Inscriptions often enable seals to be closely dated, particularly if they mention a royal name (fig. **42**); for instance, the inscriptions on the impressions of seals of the kings of Iamhad (Aleppo) as in figure **15**, have made it possible to establish the order in which they reigned and to place the texts from Tell Atchana (see p.28) in chronological order. However, it is worth emphasising that inscriptions could be added to earlier seals or recut, as for example in figure **45**.

Seals such as figure **32** are rare; it was more usual to depict one patron deity before whom the owner of the seal was led by his or her own personal god or, more often, goddess. These personal or interceding goddesses were referred to by the general term Lama. In the last two centuries of the third millennium BC, under the rule of the kings of the Third Dynasty of Ur (also known as the Ur III period), this scene became ubiquitous, and on the seals of officials the patron deity was often replaced by the deified king (fig. **33**). It also became customary from then on for the deity to be shown on the right of the scene (as seen on the impression); many of the seals which are exceptions to this rule turn out, on closer examination, to be forgeries (but see fig. **43**).

34 Modern impression of a cylinder seal of the Old Babylonian period (19th–18th century BC) depicting the interceding goddess Lama and the warrior king facing the warrior goddess Ishtar. The latter stands full-face, with one foot resting on a lion, and holds a sickle-sword and a double lion-headed mace; quivers on her back, whose straps cross over her breasts, contain arrows, the ends of which rise above each shoulder; her hair falls on to her shoulders and she wears a horned head-dress, a many-stranded necklace, and a long, belted, pleated, open skirt over a close-fitting, knee-length garment with sleeves. In the field are a clean-shaven head, a fish, three drill-holes, a star-disc and crescent, a hedgehog and a recumbent bull. A cuneiform inscription was erased, but the tips of some of the wedges can still be seen. Haematite; 2.7 × 1.4–1.5 cm (slightly concave). London, British Museum, WA 130694.

35 Modern impression of a cylinder seal of the Old Babylonian period (19th–18th century BC) depicting the interceding goddess Lama and the king in ceremonial robes, carrying an animal offering. They approach the sun god, who stands with one foot on a mountain and holds his attribute – a saw-toothed knife. Behind him, on a dais, stands a kilted priest with a forehead ornament, who holds a bucket and sprinkler. Between the central figures are a star-disc and crescent. Jaspery goethite; 2.6 × 1.4 cm. Oxford, Ashmolean Museum, 1949.894.

The first half of the second millennium BC

These centuries are generally known as the Old Babylonian period after the dynasty that ruled in Babylon from 1894 to 1595 BC and whose greatest king was Hammurabi (1792–1750 BC). During the first two centuries of the second millennium BC presentations before the deified king continued to be popular, but early on the leading goddess was replaced by a suppliant Lama with both hands raised, standing behind the owner of the seal (fig. **8**). Scenes showing the king as a warrior standing before the goddess Lama gradually superseded the presentation scenes. Although this allowed more space for an inscription, the scene did not fit well with the traditional presentation, since Lama had to turn her back on the seated deity (as in fig. **6**). Standing deities therefore became the rule, and the owner of the seal made way for representations of the king – not a specific ruler, but a symbol of the concept of kingship – either dressed in a kilt as a warrior (fig. **34**) or wearing a long ceremonial robe and often holding an animal offering (fig. **35**). These seals, almost invariably cut in haematite, are technically superb.

36 Hammer-handled Hittite stamp seal from Tarsus in Cilicia, dating to the 16th century BC. The modern impressions of the scenes carved on its base and sides show various cult scenes involving deities. Note the pointed, horned head-dress of some of the deities, which is typically Hittite; the boots with upturned toes; and the Hittite version of the Egyptian *ankh* – symbol of life (*see also* fig. **15**). The guilloche appears in even more elaborate versions than in Syria (*compare* fig. **37**). Haematite; seal height 4.25 cm. Oxford, Ashmolean Museum, 1889.318.

During the nineteenth century BC, merchants from Ashur set up trading colonies in Anatolia, of which the most important was at Kültepe. Their use of seals for sealing their business documents (fig. **13**) inspired the development of local styles. These local styles varied from centre to centre, some preferring stamp seals to cylinder seals, but all are characterised by the compulsion to fill all the available space. The seals show some assimilation of Mesopotamian themes, and frequently their reinterpretation. These seals were succeeded, around 1700 BC, by hammer-headed stamp-cylinders and four-sided stamp seals (fig. **36**) decorated with elaborate braids and guilloche patterns and showing gods wearing distinctive pointed, horned head-dresses and boots with upturned toes.

During the first half of the eighteenth century BC, trade flourished throughout northern Mesopotamia, and Mari, on the Middle Euphrates, became an important centre. The seals of officials, such as that of Ana-Sin-taklaku (fig. **11**), illustrate the development of a Syrian style incorporating Mesopotamian

37 Modern impression of a Syrian cylinder seal of the 18th century BC, which was bought in Aleppo by T. E. Lawrence. The main scene is set between two guilloche bands and consists of a goddess whose skirt falls open to reveal her nudity (*see* figs. **11** and **38**); Usimu – the two-faced vizier of the water god (*see* fig. **32**) – leads her by the hand before the enthroned water god, who has water flowing from his shoulder; there is a fish in the field. The subsidiary scene is divided into two registers by a triple guilloche; above, an ibex is attacked by a griffin; below, two ibexes lie on either side of a stylised tree. Haematite; 2.3 × 1.0 cm. Oxford, Ashmolean Museum, 1913.165.

38 Modern impression of a Syrian cylinder seal. It shows a goddess lifting the fringed corners of her skirt to reveal her nudity and a goddess wearing an Egyptian wig and head-dress and carrying two tall Egyptian loaves of bread. They approach a bearded Syrian ruler, who wears a brimmed head-dress similar to that of Mesopotamian kings and a robe with thick borders over a horizontally-striped kilt. In the field are a star, a bird, a second star and a variant on the Egyptian *ankh* – symbol of life. A subsidiary scene is divided into two registers by a guilloche band: above, two long-eared, winged demons kneel on either side of an incense burner; below is a long-eared ibex. There is a line border around the top of the seal; the lower edge is damaged and the line border is missing. Haematite; 2.15 × 1.25 cm. London, British Museum, WA 129585.

compositions and motifs blended with motifs from Egypt and Anatolia. The royal seals of the kings of Aleppo, for instance (fig. 15), show a scene related to that of the Old Babylonian king facing the goddess Lama, but both the king and the goddess wear Syrian robes with thick borders (perhaps depicting fur) and tall head-dresses. Furthermore, this Syrian goddess holds out to the king the Egyptian *ankh*, symbol of life. When she does occur, Lama is often subordinate (fig. 15). Not all Syrian goddesses are as chastely clothed, however, and seals frequently show the goddess drawing her skirt aside to reveal her nakedness (figs. 11 and 37) or holding her skirt wide open (fig. 38). In the latter case, the fringed edges of her skirt look like a skipping-rope and are often mistaken by forgers, who omit the lines showing the skirt on either side of her waist.

In contemporary Iran, a local bituminous stone was frequently substituted for haematite; it was easier to cut and the seals are not generally of such high quality. Seals showing worshippers before a king or god are common, but can be distinguished from those of Syria and Mesopotamia by several characteristics: the worshipper's hair bulges out over his forehead; he holds out his hands with one arm shown above the other (a feature also found on some seals from Sippar in Mesopotamia); and the horns on the divine head-dress flare outwards instead of curving inwards. These traits were to distinguish seals from Iran for centuries to come (fig. 41).

Technical innovation during the second half of the eighteenth century BC (see ch.4) led to the extensive use of the cutting-wheel and drill. Figures were built up around a wide central groove executed with a broad cutting-wheel, and details were added with narrower cutting-wheels and drills of varying sizes (fig. 39). Another innovation of the period, of which the first securely dated example is on Hammurabi's famous law code stele (in the Louvre, Paris), shows a perspective view of the horned head-dress worn by deities which, until this time, had been depicted frontally on a profile head; figure 39 shows both treatments of the head-dress. In this context it should be noted that frontal views are very rare throughout Ancient Near Eastern art of all periods; the nude hero (fig. 42) and the warrior goddess (figs. 32 and 34) are, for some reason, remarkably consistent exceptions to this rule.

The second half of the second millennium BC

A dark age of almost two hundred years succeeded the fall of the First Dynasty of Babylon in 1595 BC. By the end of this period the north of Syria and Mesopotamia were ruled by the Mitannians, whose faience seals (e.g. fig. **14**) rarely depicted deities. After the collapse of Mitanni in the second half of the fourteenth century BC, the Anatolian Hittites and the Egyptians vied for control of Syria and Palestine. The Hittites themselves used stamp seals, often two-sided and bearing only a Hittite hieroglyphic inscription; royal seals show the king in the embrace of a god, accompanied by inscriptions in Hittite hieroglyphs and cuneiform script. Some of the finest Syrian seals reflect these influences, but many are undistinguished and follow the general tendency to depict demons rather than deities. Under the impetus of trade, the cylinder seal was adopted on the island of Cyprus for a brief period and some very handsome seals were produced, with rows of animal-headed demons (or masked priests) – and, more rarely, deities – holding animals (fig. **40**).

39 Modern impression of a cylinder seal of the Old Babylonian period (18th–17th century BC) depicting two pairs of figures. The storm god brandishes a mace, holds a lightning fork and rests his foot on a recumbent bull; a robed king faces him and carries an animal offering. A warrior god holds a sickle-sword and a double lion-headed mace, and rests his foot on a dragon; a deity, with head-dress shown in profile and one hand raised, faces him, and between them is a sun-disc. There is a line border around the bottom of the seal. Here the design has been carefully executed with a series of small drills and cutting-wheels. Often, however, thicker wheels and drills are used, and the effect is far less attractive. The profile head-dress was an innovation c. 1760 BC; the composition, with pairs of figures, and the use of the drill point to a date after c. 1740 for the execution of this seal. Haematite with a lower, star-shaped, silver alloy ornamental cap preserved; 2.2 (2.5 with cap) × 1.05 cm. London, British Museum, WA 89477.

40 Modern impression of a Cypriote cylinder seal of the 14th century BC. Four figures hold animals up by their hind legs; one is probably male and another female, one is bull-headed or bull-masked and the other is double-lion-headed or masked. In the spaces between the figures are a bird with wings outstretched, a rosette and a fist. The composition is typical of the Cypriote Elaborate style; also typical are the full, rounded shapes of the figures, their puffed-out cheeks, and their feet with high insteps. Haematite; 2.85 × 1.15–1.3 cm (slightly concave). London, British Museum, WA 134771.

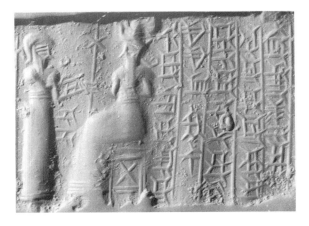

41 A worshipper faces a seated deity and stretches out both hands. Note the worshipper's bouffant hairstyle and the way his arms cross each other: both are typical of Iran, as is the god's head-dress with outward-flaring horns. The long inscription is somewhat obscure. Impure quartz; variegated brown, red and white jasper (*see* **cover illustration**); 3.65 × 1.6 cm. London, British Museum, WA 140793.

Further east, the Assyrians began to assert themselves politically; this is reflected in the beautiful seals they produced in the fourteenth and thirteenth centuries BC (figs. **3**, **26** and part of the design of **17**), but although divine symbols were depicted, deities were rarely shown except in peripheral areas. In the south, in Kassite Babylonia, although there are some exceptions (fig. **20**), typical seals are covered with long inscriptions in the form of prayers; the figures of a worshipper and god are elongated. Lengthy inscriptions and elongated style are also found on some contemporary seals from Iran (fig. **41**).

The first millennium BC

There was another dark age of some three centuries from about 1200 BC, and few seals can be dated reliably to this period. Syria and Palestine adopted the Phoenician alphabet and its variants, switching mainly to the stamp seal (see fig. **24B–C**). Occasionally the stamp-cylinder was used and this was the shape adopted in the kingdom of Urartu to the north (fig. **7**). The cylinder seal was retained, however, and with the Neo-Assyrian revival in the ninth century BC and the attendant renewed expansion in the use of cuneiform writing, it gained popularity. Unfortunately, the seals of this period are rarely inscribed, and it is therefore extremely difficult to date them. A linear style of the ninth and eighth centuries BC frequently depicts the king partaking in a ritual meal, but there are only a few representations of deities in this style. A drilled and modelled style of the early eighth century shows a variety of deities (fig.**16**), but they are not always easy to identify. A very handsome green garnet seal of about 700 BC depicts the goddess Ishtar in her warrior aspect (fig. **18**). Stamp seals show divine symbols, and the seal of the royal administration (fig. **2B**) depicts the king fighting a lion.

Contemporary Babylonian cylinder seals feature divine heroes fighting lions; gods are rarely represented, with the exception of those on large votive cylinders found at Babylon (see fig. **21**) and carved, exceptionally, in relief. It is doubtful, therefore, whether these were ever intended for sealing. Later cylinders and stamp seals mostly depict priests in front of divine symbols. Although generally the cylinders were carefully executed, the stamps were frequently reduced to a few lines and drill-holes (fig. **1D**).

Achaemenid craftsmen produced some remarkable seals from the sixth to fourth centuries BC (fig. 27), but the Zoroastrian religion precluded the representations of divine figures. The images were usually restricted to what is (debatably) a depiction of their chief god, Ahura-Mazda, within a winged disc – a motif inherited from the Assyrians. For the same reason Parthian and Sasanian seals showed divine symbols rather than the deities themselves (fig. 1E).

Other aspects of design

It has not been possible, in this brief summary of styles and iconography, to discuss various other aspects of seal design which also enable us to interpret the past. For instance, seals provide unparalleled information on changes in the types of dress from period to period and area to area, although it should be noted that deities have always tended to be conservative, continuing to dress according to fashions which their worshippers have discarded in favour of new styles. In many cases seals have provided pictorial evidence for the elevations of buildings of which only the ground-plans have survived: for instance, for the use of domes in the late fourth millennium BC. Various innovations first attested on seals include the lute in the Akkadian period (c. 2300 BC), different types of transport, and the spoked wheel. The depiction of imported, exotic species of animals, such as the water-buffalo or the Bactrian camel, indicate trade with the East; so does the adoption of the cylinder seal by some Indus Valley merchants (on the borders of Pakistan and India) from about 2300 BC. Games and sports, the earliest bull-leaping, dances and scenes from daily life, mythology, ritual and war are all recorded in great detail in these miniature reliefs.

Analysing a cylinder seal

To give some idea of the problems encountered in using seals to interpret the past, it is useful to examine one particular cylinder in some detail (fig. 42). It was excavated by Leonard Woolley at a site on the border between Turkey and western Syria, at Tell Atchana, the ancient Alalakh (see p. 28), in Room 16 of the Level IV palace. Its context would therefore date it to the fifteenth or early fourteenth century BC. However, it was made of haematite and depicts a kilted king before the goddess Lama, which would indicate a date in the Old Babylonian period. It is possible, therefore, that the seal was either a copy of an earlier seal, or it was an heirloom. In order to establish which, we need to look at the rest of the design.

First we shall examine the so-called 'filling motifs'. This term is misleading because it implies that the motifs were chosen at random to fill the spaces left after the main design had been carved. In fact, it seems that they were probably added at the express wish of the seal's purchaser, and all had a very special meaning. If we call them 'filling motifs', it is to a large extent because this meaning now eludes us. From left to right and top to bottom on the seal, the first motif is the disc within a crescent which is found during most of the second millennium BC; however, the four-pointed star within the disc would fit better in the Old Babylonian period. This seems to have been a shorthand for depicting the main astral bodies – the sun, moon and planet Venus – and alluding to the deities behind them. The demon's head is also found on Old

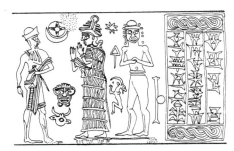

42 Cylinder seal excavated at Tell Atchana (Turkey). It depicts the king as a warrior facing the interceding goddess Lama; behind Lama is a nude hero, shown frontally, with hands clasped. In the field are a star-disc and crescent, a demon head, a bull's head, a star, a spade, a seated goat and a ball-and-staff. The three-line cuneiform inscription is set between guilloche borders: *Qarrādum, son of Iddin-Derītum, servant of Aqba-hammu*. For a detailed discussion see pp. 52–4. Haematite; 2.8 × 1.4 cm. London, British Museum, WA 126173.

Babylonian seals and is generally thought to represent the giant Humbaba, who guarded the cedars of Lebanon and was beheaded by the Mesopotamian epic hero Gilgamesh (fig. **10**, top row centre). The bull's head, with its horns seen frontally, is depicted in exactly the same way on a seal impression found in the Level VII palace at Tell Atchana (eighteenth to seventeenth century BC) and on another from a palace at Acemhöyük in central Anatolia (early to mid-eighteenth century BC); the latter impression belonged to a servant of King Aplahanda of Carchemish. Carchemish was an important trading city on the Euphrates where it crosses the border into Turkey, and Acemhöyük itself was perhaps the ancient Burushhanda, mentioned in the Cappadocian texts and also an important trading city.

At the top of the next group of motifs is a star which occurs in most periods and cannot be used as evidence for one date rather than another. The object below it is the spade or *mar* of the god Marduk – a punning symbol that may reflect his possible origins as an agricultural god. Marduk was the patron god of Babylon, so the presence of his symbol on a seal found in Syria would, at first, seem puzzling. In the circumstances, however, it makes perfect sense, as we shall see below. The little goat seated on its haunches and looking back over its shoulder is typical of Old Babylonian contest scenes, where it is shown seated on a hillock and being attacked by a lion. These contests may have had an astrological significance, but this needs further study. The final motif is the so-called ball-and-staff; this is an enigmatic object which occurs almost exclusively on seals of the Old Babylonian period. Interpretations range from a gate-post, a balance, an elixir vase, a pipe or something to do with weaving, but so far none has proved satisfactory. The conjunction of all these motifs would make an Old Babylonian date probable.

The third figure on the seal, a nude hero, is executed in a very different style from the other two figures. The use of cutting-wheel and drill are apparent, and we have seen (in ch. 4) that this innovation appeared in Babylonia in the second half of the eighteenth century BC. There is some evidence that this style of cutting may have originated even earlier in Syria and spread from there to Babylonia. A seal impression from Mari on the Middle Euphrates, well dated to shortly before the destruction of the city by Hammurabi of Babylon in 1758 BC, shows a nude goddess executed in a similar style together with the same two more traditionally Babylonian figures as are found on our seal. However, the drill and cutting-wheel were also used extensively in the second half of the second millennium BC, and the nude hero could well have been added to an heirloom Old Babylonian seal in the fifteenth century BC. Nevertheless, the arrangement of the Old Babylonian 'filling motifs' around him make it likely that the nude hero also dates from the eighteenth century BC.

Finally, let us examine the inscription. It is arranged, like most Old Babylonian inscriptions, in three lines. The guilloche borders at the top and bottom are most unusual in southern Mesopotamia but they are found on eighteenth-century seal impressions from Mari, Chagar Bazar on the river Khabur in Syria, and Tell el Rimah (possibly the ancient Karana) on the north Mesopotamian plain. All three sites shared strong commercial and political ties. The content of the inscription provides an even stronger link with these sites: it names the owner as Qarrādum – a name that occurs on tablets from all three sites. It also tells us that he was the servant of Aqba-hammu. Old Babylonian seals generally state that the owner was the servant of a god or king, and it is known from texts from Tell el Rimah that Aqba-hammu was ruler there and became a vassal of Hammurabi of Babylon.

Armed with this information, we can look once more at the design, several elements of which now acquire a new meaning. The main figures combine the seal-cutting styles of Babylonia and Syria, and this is what we would expect in an area that had contacts with both. The spade of Marduk could well have been added when Aqba-hammu went over to Hammurabi of Babylon. The Humbaba head was particularly significant at Tell el Rimah, where excavation has revealed that two such heads decorated the temple doorway. Perhaps the bull's head referred to Carchemish, a city with which Qarrādum may have been engaged in trade. However, the appearance of the bull's head on an early sealing from Tell Atchana is an interesting link with that site. How Qarrādum's seal came to be found in a much later context at Tell Atchana is something we shall probably never know.

— 6 —

The Development of Glyptic Studies

Over the last few years there has been a growing interest in seals and sealings – a field often referred to as *glyptic* studies. Whereas once museums were the main buyers, it now seems that an increasing number of private individuals are collecting seals. A few view seals primarily as an investment, but even those who start their collections with investment in mind rapidly become enthusiasts as their knowledge of seals increases.

Early interest in seals

The way the British Museum built up its collections can be taken as typical of major Western museums. Some of the first Near Eastern seals to come to Europe were acquired by private individuals (see ch. 2). These became the foundation of the Museum's collections and in 1791, when J. Tassie and R. E. Raspe published in London *A Descriptive Catalogue of a General Collection of Ancient and Modern Engraved Gems, Cameos as well as Intaglios*, at least twenty-five of the Ancient Near Eastern seals listed were in the British Museum. To this were added small numbers of seals brought back by travellers, and some major private collections built up by Claudius James Rich (see p. 22) in Mesopotamia (25 scarabs, 215 gems – not all necessarily Near Eastern – and 57 cylinder seals were purchased in 1825), Claude Scott Steuart or Stewart (203 seals purchased in 1841), and John Robert Steuart (185 seals purchased in 1846 and 1849). Most of these seals were unprovenanced, but where provenances were recorded the seals were mostly attributed either to Babylon or to one of the Assyrian sites, usually Nineveh. This probably reflects the fact that these sites are prominent in the Bible and were the ones most often visited by travellers. Thus the vast majority of seals in these early collections were Old Babylonian (*c.*1900–1600 BC) and Neo-Babylonian seals (sixth century BC), both periods when Babylon was a flourishing city. Many Neo-Assyrian examples, from the ninth to seventh centuries BC when Assyria was dominant, were also present, but there are few from Early Dynastic times (*c.*2900–2340 BC) and none then in the British Museum were from the earliest periods, as these were yet to be revealed by excavation.

Excavated seals

The seals in European collections that come from excavated sites reflect the interest of the excavators – an interest often based on political necessity. The Louvre and Bibliothèque Nationale in Paris have large collections of seals from the Levant and the site of Telloh in southern Mesopotamia. The Pergamon Museum in Berlin has material from the early site of Uruk, from Babylon and from the Assyrian capital at Ashur. The British Museum has seals brought back by Layard (figs. **9** and **25**, and see p. 22), probably mainly from his excavations at Nineveh and Nimrud, as well as a vast body of material from Leonard Woolley's excavations at Ur (figs. **10** and **19**, and see pp. 28 and 33) and some material from the work of Max Mallowan (1904–78) in the Khabur region of northern Syria. In the last few decades new antiquities laws have been enacted in the various countries of the Near East, and foreign excavators are not now usually allowed to retain any of the finds from their excavations.

Forgeries

In order to curb the illicit looting of sites, a United Nations convention was drawn up making it illegal for signatories (and their national museums) to acquire objects which had not been out of their presumed country of origin for at least fifty years. Needless to say, such a convention is not regarded as binding by most private collectors, and as a result seals are now part of a lucrative illicit traffic in antiquities and prices have soared. This has resulted in a parallel increase in the number of forgeries on the market.

Many forgers attempt to imitate known styles and generally their work is easily recognisable. It should be borne in mind, however, that even in antiquity metropolitan styles were copied by local artisans; they, too, often misunderstood what they were copying and made mistakes. For instance, forgers frequently copy a seal design from its impression in a book; the resulting design will be reversed on the faked seal. The main deity on seals from the late third millennium BC onwards is almost always shown on the right of the scene in the impression and when he or she appears on the left, this is generally a cause for suspicion. However, seal-cutters from Carchemish in the eighteenth century BC consistently reversed the direction of their designs (fig. **43**) and since the styles are varied, it is clear that this was not the quirk of one individual. Some forgers indulge in pure flights of fantasy, but the most imaginative have a real feeling for seals combined with high technical expertise, which they use to produce original works of art hard to distinguish from the work of an equally gifted craftsman in antiquity who may have refused to be fettered by the conventions of his time.

One gifted forger (fig. **44**) has combined a long narrow shape used in the early third millennium (compare fig. **25**) with a material employed one thousand years later (haematite), a basic composition found occasionally on Akkadian seals (c.2250 BC), and elements of design from various other periods. The procession of men is based on an Akkadian seal (fig. **9**); the tree is influenced by that on a Middle Assyrian seal of the thirteenth century BC (fig. **26**) and is also found on a number of inspired forgeries – probably all the work of the same person. The style is characterised by the use of a very fine drill (e.g. for the eyes, nose tip and nostrils of the figures, the drilled mane of one of

43 Modern impression of a Syrian seal of the early 18th century BC. The interceding goddess Lama faces a Syrian ruler, who wears a royal head-dress resembling that of Mesopotamian kings and a robe with ornamental borders over a horizontally-striped kilt. Between the two figures are a winged sun-disc (the disc is shaped like a rosette), a fish and a creature resembling a monkey. The inscription names the owner as *Matrunna, daughter of Aplahanda, servant-girl of the goddess Kubaba.* Aplahanda is known to have been king of Carchemish, on the Euphrates, during the early years of the 18th century BC. On this, as on other seals from Carchemish at this period, the order is reversed from what we would expect: here, for instance, the goddess is on the left and the king on the right (*compare with* figs. **34** and **42**). Haematite; 2.4 × 1.2 cm. New York, Metropolitan Museum of Art, Collection of Mrs William H. Moore, lent by Rt Rev. Paul Moore, Jr., 1955, L. 55.49.139.

44 Impression of a recent forgery of a cylinder seal combining features from a variety of periods (*see* pp. 56–7). Haematite; 5.7 cm high. On the market in London in 1983.

the lions, the eyes of the animals and birds); the upper and lower lids are clearly marked; and vegetation, animal tails, antlers and small animals are indicated by fine herringbone incisions.

Glyptic studies

The aim of Tassie and Raspe's *Descriptive Catalogue* (see p. 55) was to promote the sale of their casts of seals. When, in 1847 in Paris, Félix Lajard published more than 550 accurate engravings of Ancient Near Eastern seals from all the major collections of his day, his purpose was to illustrate his *Introduction à l'étude du culte public et des mystères de Mithra en Orient et en Occident*. Claudius James Rich's *Second Memoir on Babylon* (London, 1815) is the first objective discussion of seals. Until this time it was generally assumed that cylinder seals were talismans, but Rich pointed out that 'Some of them have cuneiform writing on them . . . but it has the remarkable peculiarity that it is reversed, or written from right to left, every other kind of cuneiform writing being incontestably to be read from left to right. This can only be accounted for by supposing they were intended to roll off impressions.' Joachim Menant, in his *Glyptique orientale* (Paris, 1883 and 1886), was the first to publish an extensive study of the seals. He was followed in 1910 by William Hayes Ward, whose *The Seal Cylinders of Western Asia* (Washington, DC, 1910) included drawings of over a thousand seals. Henri Frankfort's *Cylinder Seals* (London, 1939) was a breakthrough in glyptic studies, with its attempt at interpreting the meaning behind the designs. The most recent general study of cylinder seals is my own *First Impressions* (London, 1987; Chicago, 1988), which includes a full bibliography.

Museums gradually began to publish their seals. Among these catalogues are the first studies of stamp seals – a field which, until recently, has been much neglected. Louis Delaporte catalogued the Musée Guimet, Bibliothèque Nationale and Louvre collections in Paris between 1909 and 1923 and Pierre Bordreuil has recently produced a *Catalogue des sceaux ouest-sémitiques inscrits* (Paris, 1986). L. Speleers published the seals in the Musées Royaux d'Art et d'Histoire in Brussels in 1917 and 1943. The seals in the University Museum in Philadelphia appeared under the title *The Culture of the Babylonians* by L. Legrain (Philadelphia, 1925). The Berlin cylinder seals were catalogued by Anton Moortgat in his *Vorderasiatische Rollsiegel* (Berlin, 1940), and the stamp seals by L. Jakob-Rost (1975). Briggs Buchanan set out to publish all the Ashmolean Museum seals in Oxford: the cylinders appeared in 1966 and, after his death, P. R. S. Moorey edited the stamp seals (1984 and 1988); the first volume of Buchanan's catalogue of the seals in the Yale Babylonian Collection also appeared posthumously in 1981. The British Museum has been slower to publish. Three volumes of cylinder seals have been produced since 1962 by D. J. Wiseman and D. Collon, and the last two are in preparation. The Sasanian seals were catalogued by A. D. H. Bivar in 1969. Three volumes by M.-Th. Vollenweider on the seals of the Musée d'Art et d'Histoire in Geneva have appeared since 1967.

A number of private collections have also been published. Most of Louis De Clercq's seals were contained in the first volume of the catalogue of his collection (Paris, 1888). Lady Helena Carnegie published the collection of her father, the Earl of Southesk, in 1908. Several collections were catalogued by H. H. von der Osten (the Newell Collection in 1934, the Brett in 1936 and the von Aulock in 1957). G. A. Eisen published the Moore Collection in 1940. A landmark in the study of seals was Edith Porada's *Corpus of Near Eastern Seals in the Pierpont Morgan Library Collection* (Washington, DC, 1948). Her many articles and the seminars she has conducted have been an inspiration to scholars for several decades. More recently Beatrice Teissier has catalogued the Marcopoli Collection (Berkeley, 1984) and the auctioneers, Christie's of London, produced a copiously illustrated catalogue of the early Near Eastern stamp seals in the Erlenmeyer Collection (1989).

The first major group of excavated seals appeared in Leonard Woolley's *Ur Excavations* II; *The Royal Cemetery* (London, 1934); L. Legrain devoted two more volumes in the series to sealings and seals (1936 and 1951). Other important groups of excavated material have been discussed by T. Beran, H. Güterbock and R. M. Boehmer (Boğazköy), A. Moortgat and T. Beran (Ashur), E. Porada (Nuzi, Choga Zanbil, Enkomi), H. Frankfort (the Diyala), N. Özgüç (Kültepe), S. Alp (Karahöyük/Konya), P. Amiet (Susa), D. Collon (Tell Atchana/Alalakh), M. Brandes (Uruk), P. Kjaerum (Failaka), C. Schaeffer-Forrer (Ras Shamra/Ugarit and Enkomi), H. Martin (Fara) and D. Beyer (Emar).

Some periods have been investigated in special monographs: P. Amiet's *Glyptique mésopotamienne archaïque* (Paris, 1961 and 1980) dealt with seals up to and including the Early Dynastic Period, R. M. Boehmer treated the Akkadian period in *Die Entwicklung der Glyptik während der Akkad-Zeit* (Berlin, 1966), and L. al-Gailani Werr's *Studies in the Chronology and Regional Style of Old Babylonian Cylinder Seals* (Malibu) appeared in 1988. A major three-volume work entitled *Studies on Scarab Seals*, by W. A. Ward and O. Tufnell, was published in Warminster between 1978 and 1984, and further studies on Levantine glyptic are appearing under the aegis of O. Keel of Fribourg University in Switzerland. Certain iconographical features have been extensively discussed, for instance in C. Kepinski's *L'arbre stylisé en Asie occidentale au 2ᵉ millénaire avant J.-C.* (Paris, 1982).

Various aspects of seal use have been the focus of recent studies, such as the legal use of seals, and the study of the backs of sealings to establish what materials they accompanied. The function of seals was the subject of a symposium organised by McG. Gibson and R. D. Biggs in Chicago; the papers were published in 1977 as *Seals and Sealing in the Ancient Near East* (Malibu).

Special exhibitions of seals have also been organised, of which the most imaginative was held at the Paris mint in 1973. The designs on seals were enlarged so that they appeared as full-scale relief sculptures. The exhibition was entitled *Bas-reliefs imaginaires* and was supported by a well-illustrated catalogue by P. Amiet.

This list is, perforce, selective in the extreme. The authors referred to above, and many others too numerous to mention, have also produced articles and monographs on various groups of seals or aspects of glyptic studies. However, this short book will have achieved its purpose if readers are inspired to look at the seals themselves (e.g. fig. **45**) with renewed interest and to find out more about them.

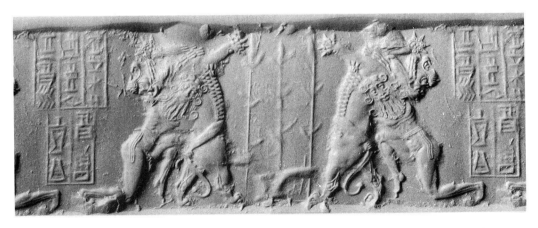

45 Modern impression of a cylinder seal of the Akkadian period (*c.* 2250 BC), carved with antithetical groups of contestants, in each case a hero wrestling with a lion. The hero is bearded and wears his hair in three curls on either side of his face. He kneels on one knee and has wrapped one arm round the lion's neck, which he bends back over his shoulder; with the other arm he encircles the lion's body and grasps its tail. Despite the small size of the seal, and the hard striped stone from which it was cut (*see* **cover illustration**), the seal-cutter has even succeeded in differentiating between the backs and pads of the lion's paws. The contestants frame an inscription: *Puzur-Shullat, priest of* BAD: *Shakullum, the scribe, is your servant*. Another inscription was erased and rushes were carved instead. Red-and-white-striped jasper with bevelled edges; 3.6 × 2.3 cm. London, British Museum, WA 89147.

Chronological Table

5000 BC	Halaf Period
	Ubaid Period (fig. **1A**)
4000 BC	
	Uruk Period (figs. **1B, 2A, 4, 5, 28, 29**)
3000 BC	
	Early Dynastic Period (figs. **12, 19, 25, 30, 31**)
2334 BC	
	Akkadian Period (figs. **9, 32, 45**)
2212 BC	
	Ur III Period (fig. **33**)
2000 BC	
	Old Babylonian Period (figs. **1C, 6, 8, 11, 13, 15, 17, 22–4A, 34–9, 42, 43**)
1595 BC	
1500 BC	
	Kassite / Middle Assyrian / Mitannian Period (figs. **3, 14, 17, 20, 26, 40, 41**)
1200 BC	
1000 BC	
	Neo-Assyrian Period (figs. **2B, 7, 10, 16, 18, 24B–C**)
612 BC	
	Neo-Babylonian Period (figs. **1D, 10, 21**)
539 BC	
	Achaemenid Persian Empire (figs. **10, 27**)
331 BC	Beginning of Greek rule (Alexander the Great)
250 BC	
	Parthians in the East
AD 224	
	Sasanian Empire (fig. **1E**)
AD 651	Islamic Period

Index of Figure References

Numerals in bold type indicate figure numbers and cross-references to illustrations within figure captions.
For the current location of the seals see p. 7; for their chronological distribution see opposite.

1A 11, 14, 39
  B 11, 40
  C 11, 38
  D 11, 41, 51
  E 11, 42, 52
2A 11
  B 19, 25, 41, 51
3 11, 40, 51
4 11, 14, 19, 26, 33
5 15
6 15, 36, 47
7 17, 51
8 19, 21, 47
9 22, 31, 56
10 25, 53, 56
11 19, 25, 48, 49; **8, 37**
12 24, 26
13 11, 26, 48

14 27, 28, 40, 50
15 11, 28, 49; **36**
16 30, 41, 51
17 19, 30, 40, 51
18 32, 41, 44, 51
19 33, 44, 56
20 35, 46, 51
21 11, 35, 51
22 37; **23**
23 37
24A 37
  B 37, 41, 51
  C 21, 31, 37, 41, 51
25 37, 56
26 19, 40, 51, 56; **8**
27 30, 41, 52
28 43
29 43

30 44
31 44
32 31, 44–6, 49; **9, 37**
33 46; **13**
34 44, 47, 49; **43**
35 44, 47
36 48
37 46, 49; **36**
38 49; **37**
39 49
40 50
41 49, 51
42 46, 49, 52–4; **17, 43**
43 46, 56
44 56
45 46, 59

Index

Numbers in bold type refer to illustrations and captions

abrasive 39–40
Abu Salabikh 24
Acemhöyük (Burushhanda?) 26, 53
Achaemenid Persians 18, 21, 25, 35, 41, 52; 10, 27
Adad-nirari I 3
Adad-sharrum 11
Adda 32
Aegean 17, 40
Afghanistan 26, 30, 32; 1C, 12
Africa 32
agate 31, 35, 40
Akkad, Akkadian 16, 21, 31, 33, 40, 44, 52, 56, 59; 9, 32, 45
Alalakh *see* Atchana
Aleppo (Iamhad) 28, 46, 49; 15, 37
Alexander the Great 35
al-Gailani Werr, L. 59
Alp, S. 58
alphabet *see* writing
Amarna, Tell el- 34–5
amethyst 31, 37
Amiet, P. 7, 58–9
Ammenemes II 33
Amu Darya *see* Oxus
amulet 9, 21, 39; 1B
Anatolia 12, 16–17, 26, 34, 48–50, 53; 13; *see also* Turkey
Ana-Sin-taklaku 25, 48; 11
ankh 49; 15, 23, 36, 38
antelope 14
Aplahanda 26, 53; 43
Aqba-hammu 54; 42
Araba 12
Aratta 33
Arikamedu 42
Arpachiyah 39
Arzawa 34
Ashur 22, 26, 48, 56, 58
Ashur-rimanni 26
Ashur-uballit I 34; 17
Asmar, Tell (Eshnunna) 8
Assyria, Assyrian 16, 22, 25–6, 31–2, 34–5, 40, 41, 44, 51–2, 55–6; 10, 13, 17, 21
  Old Assyrian 26, 48, 53; 13
  Middle Assyrian 31, 51, 56; 3, 17, 26
  Neo-Assyrian 21, 51, 55; 2B, 10, 16, 18
astral symbol *see* moon, star, sun
astrology 53
Atchana, Tell (Alalakh) 7, 28, 46, 52–3, 58; 14, 15, 42

Babylon 22, 35, 47, 53–6; 9, 21, 33
Babylonia, Babylonian 16, 22,

25, 32, 34–5, 40, 41, 51, 54; 20, 21
  Old Babylonian 44, 47, 49, 50, 52–5, 59; 6, 8, 11, 34, 35, 39, 42
  Neo-Babylonian 21, 55; 1D, 10, 21
Bactria 52; 1C
Badakhshan 32
Baghdad 22
  Iraq Museum 7; 3, 10
Bahrein 1C, 25
ball, clay 15; 5
ball-and-staff 53; 23, 42
banquet 43–4; 19
Beran, T. 58
beryl 31
Berlin, Antikenmuseum 7; 16
  Pergamonmuseum 7, 22, 56, 58; 21, 29, 30
Beyer, D. 58
Biggs, R. D. 59
Bilalama 8
bird 37, 56; 11, 16, 22, 23, 24B, 37, 40, 44
bird-demon 31
bison 31
bituminous stone 49
Bivar, A. D. H. 58
boar 5
Bodrum 7; 17
Boehmer, R. M. 58, 59
Boğazköy 58
bone 11
Bordreuil, P. 58
Botta, P.-E. 22
bow 9, 32
bow drill *see* drill
Brak, Tell 37
Brandes, M. 58
Brett Collection 58
bronze 33, 40; 8, 16
Brussels, M. R. A. H. 58
Buchanan, B. 58
bull 52–4; 2A, 24B, 30–34, 39, 40, 42
bulla 9, 11, 17, 19, 21, 26; 2, 4, 12
Buqras 14
burial 23–4, 27–8, 33; 10, 19
Burnaburiash II 35; 20
Burushhanda *see* Acemhöyük
Buzuran 37; 23
Byblos 36

camel 52
cameo 11, 21
Cappadocian 53; *see* Old Assyrian
Carchemish 26, 53; 24B, 43
Carnegie, Lady H. 58
Carthage 37
Caspian 26–7

Çatal Hüyük 14
Caylus, Count de 21
Chagar Bazar 54
chalcedony 32, 40, 41; 1D, 16, 26, 27
Chicago, Oriental Institute 7; 8
chlorite 31–2, 36
Choga Zanbil 58
Chosroes II Parviz 42
Christies 58
Cilicia 36
clay 11, 14–17, 19–20; 2–5, 10, 12, 13, 15
Collon, D. 58
contest 43, 51, 53; 31, 45
copper 40; 29
cornelian 31, 32, 35, 40, 41; 1E
crescent *see* moon
Crete 37
Crusader 21
cuneiform *see* writing
cutting-wheel 40–41, 49, 54; 39
cylinder seal 15–19, 21, 24, 26, 30, 34, 39–41, 50–52; 2A, 3, 5, 6, 8–23, 25–27, 29–36, 38–45
Cyprus, Cypriote 17, 29, 34–5, 37; 40

Darish-libur 11
De Clercq, L. *see* Paris
deer 57; 26, 44
Değirmentepe 14
deity *see* god, goddess
demon 50, 52; 31, 38, 40?, 42
Dhekelia 29
diamond 42
diorite 31; 9
Diyala 12; 8
dog 4
dome 52
dragon 39
drill 39–41, 49, 51, 54, 56; 1B, 17, 39

Early Dynastic 33, 43, 46, 55, 59; 12, 19, 25, 30, 31
Egypt, Egyptian 17, 21, 22, 25, 30, 33–4, 37, 41, 49–50; 22, 23, 36, 38
Eisen, G. A. 58
Elam, Elamite 16
Emar 58
Enkidu 10
Enkomi 29, 58
Enmerkar 33
enstatite 37
Erlenmeyer Collection 58
Esagila 21
Esarhaddon 21
Eshnunna *see* Asmar, Tell
Eski Mosul 31

Euphrates 11, 12, 22, 25, 26, 33, 37, 48, 54; **11, 23, 43**

faience 11, 27–9, 40, 50; **14**
Failaka 27, 38, 58; **1C**
Fara 24
filling motifs 52
fish **16, 34, 37, 43**
fist **40**
flint 39
flute **31**
fly **6?**
forgery 46, 56–7; **44**
fox **1B**
Frankfort, H. 58

garnet 32, 41, 51; **18**
Gawra, Tepe 14, 31, 33
gazelle **11**
gem 18, 21, 22, 42; **10**
gem-cutter *see* seal-cutter, jeweller
Geneva, Musée d'Art et d'Histoire 58
Gezer **24A**
Gibson, McG. 59
Gilgamesh 53; **10**
Giyan, Tepe **1A**
glass 11, 34, 40, 41
glyptic 11, 18, 55, 59
goat 53; **1C, 3, 5, 11, 42**
god, goddess 43–54, 56 and *passim*
god, Adad 21
  Ahura-Mazda 52; **27**
  Amurru **6**
  fertility **30**
  Horus **22, 23**
  hunting 44; **31, 32**
  Iranian **41**
  Marduk 53, 54; **21**
  Ninshubur **11**
  storm **21, 39**
  sun 44; **32, 35**
  Tishpak **8**
  Usimu **32, 37**
  water 44, 46; **20, 32, 37**
  warrior **11, 39**
goddess, Anahita 30
  Hera 30; **16**
  Egyptian **38**
  Inanna 43, 44; **29**
  Ishtar 44, 51; **18, 32, 34**
  Kubaba **43**
  Lama 47, 49, 52, 54; **6, 8, 11, 15, 17, 33–35, 42, 43**
  naked, nude 49, 54; **11, 37, 38**
  Syrian 49; **15**
  Venus 44, 52
  warrior 44, 49, 51; **16, 18, 31, 32, 34**
goethite 40; **35**
gold 21, 30, 34; **8, 24C, 31**
Golgotha 21
Gorelick, L. 39
Greece, Greek 18, 21, 22, 25, 27, 34, 42; **10, 20**
greenstone 31, 37; **24C, 32, 33**
guilloche 37, 48, 54; **14, 22, 23, 36–38, 42**
Gulf 12, 22, 27, 38; **1C**
Güterbock, H. 58
Gwinnett, J. 39

haematite 26, 31, 40, 41, 47, 49, 52, 56; **6, 11, 17, 24B, 34, 36–40, 42–44**
Halaf 39
Hamilton, W. 21
Hammurabi 47, 49, 54
Hasanlu 29
Hash-hammer **33**
Hazor 29
hedgehog **34**
Herakles **10**
Herzfeld, E. **1A**
hieroglyphic *see* writing
Hillah **9**
Hittite 16, 34, 50
Holy Land 21
Humbaba 53, 54; **10, 42**
Hurrian 16

Iamhad *see* Aleppo
Iarim-Lim **15**
Iaush-Addu **23**
ibex **18, 37, 38**
Ibni-Amurru **6**
Idalion 29
Iddin-Derītum **42**
Ilima-ahi **6**
Imeny **24A**
impression 9, 11, 16, 19–20 and *passim*
incense burner **38**
India, Indian 22, 29, 35, 42, 52; **1C**
Indus 11, 38, 52
inscription *see* writing
intaglio 11; **21**
Iran 12, 15, 16, 26, 27, 29, 34, 37, 43, 49, 51; **1A, 1C, 12, 28, 41**
Iraq 12, 14, 26, 29, 34; **1C, 2, 3, 8–10, 12, 19, 30, 33;** *see also* Mesopotamia
Ishkun-Sin **33**
Islam 9
ivory 11

jadeite 31
Jakob-Rost, L. 58
jasper 31, 36–7, 40, 41; **22, 23, 24C, 45**
jeweller, jewellery 19, 21, 33–5, 42; **8, 10, 18, 24C**
Jordan 12

Kalki **9**
Kamid el Loz 29
Kanesh *see* Kültepe
Karana *see* Rimah, Tell el
Karun 12
Kaş 30; **17**
Kashmir 32; **18**
Kassite 31, 35, 40, 51; **20**
Keel, O. 59
Kepinski, C. 59
Kerkha 12
Khabur 54, 56
Khorsabad 22
Kidin-Marduk **20**
Kirikiri **8**
Kjaerum, P. 58
king 19, 44, 47, 49, 51, 52, 54; **2B, 6, 8, 9, 11, 15, 17, 20, 23, 24A, 29, 33–35, 38, 39, 42, 43**

Kish 33
Kültepe 26, 48, 58; **13**

Lajard, F. 57
lapis lazuli 31–5; **8, 19, 20, 21**
Layard, A. H. 26, 56; **9, 25**
Lawrence, T. E. **37**
Lebanon, Lebanese 29, 36, 53
Legrain, L. 58
Leiden **26**
lens 42
Levant 17, 34, 56, 59
lightning **21, 38**
limestone 30, 36, 39
lion 44, 51, 53, 57; **2, 10, 18, 24B, 31, 34, 40, 45**
lion-griffin **17, 21**
London, British Museum 7, 21, 22, 31, 32, 55, 56, 58; **1, 2, 4, 6, 7, 9, 10, 12–15, 18, 19, 24, 25, 27, 32–34, 38–42, 45**
  Institute of Archaeology 7; **15**
Lothal **1C**
lute 52
Lycia 30

mace **34, 39**
magnification 42
Mallowan, M. 56
Marcopoli Collection 58
Marathon 22
marble **29**
Mari 25, 26, 33, 37, 48, 54; **11, 23**
Marlik 27
materials *see* agate, amethyst, beryl, bituminous stone, bone, bronze, chalcedony, chlorite, clay, copper, cornelian, diamond, diorite, enstatite, faience, flint, garnet, gem, glass, goethite, gold, greenstone, haematite, ivory, jadeite, jasper, lapis lazuli, limestone, marble, metal, obsidian, quartz, rock-crystal, ruby, serpentine, shell, silver, steatite, stone, turquoise, wood
Matrunna **43**
Menant, J. 57
Mesopotamia 12, 14–17, 21, 22, 26, 27, 31, 33, 34, 38, 39, 41, 43, 44, 46, 48–50, 53–6; **10, 25;** *see also* Iraq
metal 11
Mitanni, Mitannian 27–9, 34, 50; **14**
Mohammed Arab, Tell 29; **3**
monkey **22, 23, 31, 43**
monster **7, 17**
moon 52; **1E, 7, 8, 16, 17, 27, 31, 33, 35, 42**
Moore Collection 58; **43**
Moorey, P. R. S. 58
Moortgat, A. 58
Mosul 22
myopia 42
Mycenae, Mycenaean **27, 34**

Napoleon 22
Naxos 40

Nefertiti 30
Newell Collection 58
New York, Metropolitan
    Museum of Art 7; **43**
    Pierpont Morgan Library 58
    Jonathan P. Rosen Collection
        7; **23**
Nile 11, 33
Nimrud 22, 56
Nineveh 14, 22, 24, 55, 56; **2**, **4**,
    25
'Ninevite 5' style **25**
Niqmepuh **15**
nude hero 49, 54; **31**, **42**, **45**
Nuzi 28, 58

obsidian 31, 37; **23**
Old Persian 16
Oxford, Ashmolean Museum 7,
    58; **35–37**
Oxus, Oxus Treasure 30; **27**
Özgüç, N. 58

Pakistan 32, 52
Palermo 21
Palestine 12, 50, 51; **24A**
Paris, Bibliothèque Nationale 7,
    21, 56, 58; **26**
    Louvre 7, 22, 49, 56, 58; **5**, **11**,
        28, **31**
    Musée Guimet 58
Parthian 18, 42, 52
perforation 15, 39–40
Persepolis, Persepolitan 35
Persia see Iran
Persian see Achaemenid Persian,
    Old Persian
Philadelphia, University
    Museum 7, 58; **10**
Phoenicia, Phoenician 17, 37;
    24C
Pleiades 16
Porada, E. 7, 58
presentation 46–7; **33**
priest, priestess 44, 50, 51; **1D**,
    10, **17**, **19**, **29**, **30**, **35**
prisoner **5**
Pu-abi **19**
Puzur-Shullat **45**

Qarrādum 54; **42**
quartz 30–32, 41; **41**
queen **19**
Quetta 32
quiver **9**, **18**, **32**, **34**

Raspe, R. E. 55, 57
Rassam, H. 22
Ras Shamra (Ugarit) 29
recut, re-used 19, 25, 30, 34, 40,
    46; **11**, **17**, **34**, **45**
Red Sea 22
rhomb **16**
Rich, C. J. 22, 55, 57
Rimah, Tell el (Karana?) 54
rock-crystal 31
Roman 18, 21, 42
rosette **7**, **11**, **17**, **40**, **43**

ruby 42

Samarra 31
Samos 30; **16**
Sargon of Akkad 44; **9**
Sasanian 18, 32, 42, 52, 58; **1E**
Schaeffer-Forrer, C. 58
scarab, scaraboid 30, 31, 37, 41,
    59; **24**
scorpion-man **31**
scribe **9**, **32**, **45**
seal passim
seal-cutter 32
sealing **9**, 11, 17, 19, 24, 26, 27,
    54 and passim; **2**, **4**, **5**, **8**, **10**, **12**,
    28, **31**
serpentine 31, 32, 36, 41
Sha-ilimma-damqa **20**
Shahr-i-Sokhta 26; **12**
Shakullum **45**
Shamaiatum **11**
Shamshi-Adad 26
sha-reshi official **20**
sheep **29**, **30**
shell 31
Shumu-eṭir-Ashur **26**
Sidon 34
Sicily 21
silver **31**, **39**
Sippar 49
Southesk, Earl of 58
spade 53–4; **42**
Spain 27
Speleers, L. 58
sphinx **22**, **23**
stamp-cylinder 17, 26, 48, 51; **7**
stamp seal 14–19, 24, 26, 30, 31,
    34, 39–41, 48, 50, 51, 58; **1**, **2B**,
    4, **10**, **28**, **36**
star 52; **7**, **8**, **17**, **31**, **34**, **35**, **38**,
    42
steatite 31, 37; **1C**, **24A**, **25**
Steuart (or Stewart), C. S. 55
Steuart, J. R. 55
stone see materials
Sumer, Sumerian 15–16
sun 52; **7**, **8**, **11**, **16**, **17**, **24B**, **27**,
    31, **34**, **35**, **39**, **42**, **43**; see also
    god
Susa 15, 37, 43, 44, 58; **1C**, **5**, **28**,
    31
sword 11, 17, 18, **34**, **39**
Syria 12, 14, 16, 25, 26, 28, 29,
    34, 36, 37, 40, 41, 44, 48–54, 56;
    11, **14**, **15**, **22**, **23**, **24B-C**, **36–38**,
    42, **43**
tablet **9**, 11, 14, 16, 17, 19, 24,
    26–8, 34; **3**, **9**, **13**, **15**, **23**, **26**
Taip-Depe 26
Tarsus **36**
Tassie, J. 55, 57
Teheran 25; **11**
Teissier, B. 58
tell 22–3
Telloh 56
temple 33, 35, 43, 46; **30**
Thebes (Egypt) 33

Thebes (Greece) 7, 34–5; **20**
Third Dynasty of Ur see Ur III
Tigris 11, 12, 22, 40
Tod 33
token 15
trade 9, 11, 14, 15, 17, 26, 27, 29,
    32, 33, 35–8, 44, 50, 52, 54
tree 56, 59; **3**, **14**, **18**, **20**, **26**, **37**,
    44
Tufnell, O. 59
Tukulti-Ninurta I 35
Turkey 12, 14, 16, 26, 28, 30, 52,
    53; **7**, **13–17**, **24B**, **42**; see also
    Anatolia
Turkmenistan 27
turquoise 31–2

Ubil-Eshtar **9**
Ugarit see Ras Shamra
Ulu Burun 30; **17**
Umma 30
Ur 24, 26, 33, 35, 56, 58; **1C**, **10**,
    12, **19**, **33**
Ur III 46; **33**
Urals 32; **18**
Urartu, Urartian 16, 51; **7**
Ur-nammu **33**
Uruk 15, 33, 43, 56, 58; **1B**, **2A**,
    29

Victory **10**
Vélez-Málaga 27
Veronese, F. B. 21
Vollenweider, M.-L. 58
von Aulock Collection 58
von der Osten, H. H. 58

Ward, W. A. 59
Ward, W. H. 58
Warum **8**
was sceptre **22**, **23**
water-buffalo 52
wheel 52; **16**
Wilde, J. de 21
winged (sun) disc 52; **16**, **24B**,
    27, **36**, **43**
Wiseman, D. J. 58
wood 11
Woolley, C. L. 28, 33, 52, 56, 58
worshipper **1D**, **8**, **13**, **16**, **30**, **31**
writing 11, 14–19
    alphabetic 17, 18, 41, 51
    cuneiform 16, 17, 34, 35, 46,
        50, 51, 54, 57; **6**, **8**, **9**, **11**, **13**,
        15, **17**, **19–21**, **23**, **26**, **31–34**,
        41–43
    hieroglyphic 16, 37, 50; **22**,
        24A

Yale, Babylonian Collection 58
Yellow River 11
Yunus **24B**

Zab 12
Zimri-Lim 26; **11**
Zoroastrian 52; **27**